ROCK, POP, and CLASSIC CINEMA POSTERS

Auction
Sunday, 15 December 1996 at 4.00p.m. & 6.00p.m.
Murray Feldman Gallery, Pacific Design Center
8687 Melrose Avenue
Los Angeles, CA 90069

Telephone prior to exhibition: (212) 606 0543 or (310) 275 5534
Telephone during the exhibition and sale: (310) 657 1003
Fax during the exhibition and sale (310) 657 1881

Sale Code
In sending written bids or making enquiries,
this sale should be referred to as 7943

Viewing in Los Angeles
Murray Feldman Gallery, Pacific Design Center, 8687 Melrose Avenue

Thursday	12 December	12.00p.m.-7.00p.m.
Friday	13 December	12.00p.m.-7.00p.m.
Saturday	14 December	10.00a.m.-5:00p.m.

*Free Collectibles Appraisal Day on Saturday, December 14th, 11.00a.m.-4.00p.m.

Cover photo lots: 338, 586
Back Cover lots: 527, 445

Christie's Los Angeles
342 N. Rodeo Drive
Beverly Hills, CA 90210
Telephone: (310) 275 5534
Fax: (310) 275 9748
Internet: http://www.christies.com

(??) Registered at the above address No. 1128160

AUCTION PRACTICE AT CHRISTIE'S LOS ANGELES

Two years after opening their Park Avenue saleroom, Christie's headed east and found an excellent location at which to establish their "middle market" saleroom.

The former car garage offered the perfect site—with its two large freight elevators, steel-reinforced floors and 20-foot-high ceilings. With a start up team of 23 people, an exciting auction site (with an emphasis on affordability and informality) was created seemingly overnight.

Our inaugural auction in 1979 was a sale of antique and modern jewelry totaling $130,000. Less than ten years later, Christie's East saw its first million dollar sale with the 19th century collection of decorative arts from the Estate of Susana W. Lacayo. Some of the most well-known auctions of the past decade have been held at Christie's East, including the Estate of Cecil B. deMille, the Couture Collection of Tina Chow, property from the Estate of Clark Gable, and the Barbra Streisand sale.

Today, Christie's East averages 60 sales a year in over 20 different categories. With almost monthly sales of jewelry and furniture & decorative arts, there is always something "on the block." Our average lot value of $2,400 means one can find "treasures" at virtually any price range. And for those just beginning to buy at auction, our Collectibles sales may ease auction jitters: even the youngest of collectors can start by bidding on anything from lunch boxes and Hollywood posters to animation cels and antique dolls.

Christie's Los Angeles welcomes you to our viewing galleries and salerooms. Our specialists and Client Services staff will be pleased to help you with any aspect of buying or selling at auction.

THE BUYER

USING THIS CATALOGUE

Estimate Prices

In addition to descriptive information, each entry in this catalogue includes a price range which reflects the opinion of our specialists as to the price expected at auction. These are based upon prices recently paid at auction for comparable property and take into account condition, rarity, quality and history of previous ownership (provenance). Estimates are prepared well in advance of the sale and are subject to revision; they do not include the buyer's premium or sales tax. (See under separate heading.)
Where "Estimate on Request" appears, please contact the specialist department for further information.

Reserves

The reserve is the minimum price the seller is willing to accept and below which a lot will not be sold. This amount is confidential and will not exceed the low pre-sale estimate. Property offered for sale subject to a reserve is identified by the symbol • next to the lot number.

Conditions of Sale and Limited Warranty

Before you bid, we encourage you to read the **Conditions of Sale** and **Limited Warranty** which appear on the immediately following pages. The **Conditions of Sale** outline the terms governing the purchase of all property sold at auction. The **Limited Warranty** specifies the terms and conditions upon which Christie's guarantees the authenticity of property offered for sale.

Owned or Guaranteed Property

Christie's generally offers property consigned by others for sale at public auction. Occasionally, lots are offered which have in the course of the sale process become the property of Christie's. These lots are identified with the symbol ◆ next to the lot number.

Buyer's Premium and Sales Tax

Buyers are reminded that the actual purchase price will be the sum of the final bid price plus the buyer's premium, in general 15% of the first $50,000 and 10% of the excess of the hammer price above $50,000; for coins, the premium is a flat 10% of the final bid price regardless of the amount of the successful bid.

In addition to the purchase price, buyers are required to pay any sales or use tax which may be due. These charges are explained in detail under "Christie's Charges and Sales Tax" towards the end of this catalogue.

BEFORE THE AUCTION

You can attend pre-sale viewings for all our auctions at no charge. All property to be auctioned is usually on view for several days prior to the sale. You are encouraged to examine lots thoroughly and to request condition reports (see below). Christie's specialists and customer service staff are available to give advice at all viewings or by appointment.

Hours of Business

Christie's Park Avenue galleries and Christie's East are open from 10 a.m. to 5 p.m. on weekdays. During the auction seasons there is frequent weekend viewing from 10 a.m. to 5 p.m. on Saturdays and varying afternoon hours on Sundays. The viewing schedule for each sale is published in the front of the auction catalogue.

Condition Reports

If you would like additional information on a particular lot, or cannot come to the viewing, Christie's will be pleased to provide, upon request, a condition report. Please contact the specialist department in charge of the sale.

We remind prospective buyers that descriptions of property are not warranties and that each lot is sold "as is" in accordance with the terms of the **Limited Warranty.** Condition reports are provided as a service to interested clients, but the information furnished does not negate or modify the **Limited Warranty.** Neither Christie's nor the seller makes any express or implied warranty or representation as to the condition of any lot offered for sale, and no statement made at any time, whether oral or written, shall constitute such a warranty or representation.

Registration

If you are planning to bid at auction, you will need to register with us. Please arrive 20 or 30 minutes before the sale to complete bidder registration and to receive a numbered paddle to identify you if you are the successful bidder. If you are a new client, or if you have not made a recent purchase at Christie's, you may be asked to supply a bank reference when you register. To avoid any delay in the release of your purchases, you may wish to prearrange check or credit approval. If so, please contact Christie's East Credit Department at (212) 606 0466 or by fax at (212) 737 6076.

THE AUCTION

All auctions are open to the public, free of charge. You do not have to bid or register for a paddle.

Bidding

Property is auctioned in consecutive numerical order, as it appears in the catalogue. The lot being offered is usually shown at the front of the saleroom or is illustrated on a monitor. The auctioneer will accept bids from those present in the saleroom or absentee bidders participating by telephone or by written bid left with Christie's in advance of the auction. The auctioneer may also execute bids on behalf of the consignor to protect the reserve, either by placing consecutive bids up to the amount of the reserve or by entering bids in response to saleroom, telephone or absentee bids. Under no circumstances will the auctioneer place any bid on behalf of the consignor at or above the reserve. Nor will the auctioneer specifically identify bids placed on behalf of the consignor to protect the reserve.

Bidding Increments

Bidding generally opens below the low estimate and advances in the following increments:

$100 to $200	by $10
$200 to $300	by $20
$300 to $500	by $20 or $20-$50-$80
$500 to $1,000	by $50
$1,000 to $2,000	by $100
$2,000 to $3,000	by $200
$3,000 to $5,000	by $200 or $200-500-800
$5,000 to $10,000	by $500
$10,000 to $20,000	by $1,000
$20,000 to $30,000	by $2,000
$30,000 to $50,000	by $2,000 or $2000-5000-8000
$50,000 to $100,000	by $5,000
$100,000 and up	by $10,000

Occasionally the auctioneer may vary the increments during the course of the auction at his or her discretion.

Currency Conversion

Christie's may, as a convenience to bidders, use a currency conversion board during the auction to display the amounts being bid converted into several foreign currencies. These converted amounts are approximations only and may not represent the exact exchange rate at any given time.

Absentee Bids

If you cannot attend an auction, you may bid in other ways. The most common is the absentee bid, sometimes called an "order bid." Absentee bids are written instructions from you directing Christie's to bid for you on one or more lots up to a maximum amount you specify for each lot. Christie's staff will execute your absentee bid at the lowest possible price taking into account the reserve price and other bids. There is no charge for this service. If identical bids are left by two or more parties, the first bid received by Christie's will take preference. The auctioneer may execute bids for absentee bidders directly from the podium, clearly identifying these as order bids. Absentee Bid Forms are available in the back of every auction catalogue and also may be obtained at any Christie's location.

Telephone Bids

Christie's will also execute your bids if you cannot come to the auction and wish to participate by telephone. Arrangements should be confirmed at least one day in advance of the sale with Christie's East Bid Department at (212) 606 0448. Christie's staff will execute telephone bids from designated areas in the sale-room. This service is also free of charge.

Successful Bids

The fall of the auctioneer's hammer indicates the final bid. Christie's will record the paddle number of the buyer. If your saleroom or absentee bid is successful, you will be notified immediately after the sale by mailed invoice. If you are unsuccessful, Christie's Bid Department will notify you by letter.

Unsold Lots
If a lot does not reach the reserve, it is bought-in. In other words, it remains unsold and is returned to the consignor. When the auctioneer hammers down a lot that fails to sell, he will so indicate by announcing that the lot has been "passed," "withdrawn," "returned to owner" or "bought-in."

The Glossary
Terms used in this catalogue have the meanings ascribed to them below. Please note that all statements in this catalogue as to Authorship are made subject to the provisions of the CONDITIONS OF SALE, LIMITED WARRANTY and ABSENCE OF OTHER WARANTIES.

SPECIAL GLOSSARY TO CINEMA POSTERS
LOBBY CARD–11 x 14 in., heavy board stock. Originally made in sets of eight. Most sets have one title card which gives production credits and may be primarily artwork. The other seven cards are colored photographic scenes. Few intact sets survive.

WINDOW CARD–22 x 14 in., heavy board stock.Has blank area at top of card, where theatres would place their name and playdates.

HALF-SHEET–22 x 28 in., heavy stock. Most often with a horizontal and a vertical fold.

INSERT–36 x 14in., heavy stock. Most often found with two horizontal folds.

ONE-SHEET–41 x 27 in., (approximate), paper stock. Virtually always found with two horizontal folds and one vertical fold.

THREE SHEET–81 x 41 in. (approximate), paper stock. Printed on two or three separate sheets, designed to overlap. As these were often posted on walls, they are much rarer than one sheets. Very few survive from the pre-1940 period.

SIX-SHEET–81 x 81 in. (approximate), paper stock. Printed on four separate sheets, designed to overlap. As these were almost always posted on walls, they are even rarer than three sheets. Very few survive from the pre-1940 period.

24-SHEET–106 x 234 in., paper stock. Billboard poster. Very few have survived.

BRITISH QUAD–30 x 40 in., paper stock.

OTHER FOREIGN POSTERS–Varying sizes, depending on country of origin, paper stock.

LINEN BACKED–Poster has been mounted onto Japanese rice paper and then onto linen, in most cases.

PAPER BACKED–Poster has been mounted onto Japanese rice paper.

Condition Glossary for Cinema Posters
For unrestored posters:

Condition A: Above Average
Posters have bright colors and are generally free from defects but may have small tears (usually along the folds) and very small areas of paper loss that do not materially affect the image, and are easily restored.

Condition B: Average– Posters are in average used condition. They may have minor defects, including some of the following: tears, slight paper loss, minor staining, slight fading, tape on the reverse.

Condition C: Below Average—
Posters have substantial defects, including some of the following: substantial staining or paper loss, much tape on the reverse.

For restored posters:

Condition A: Posters have bright colors and *minor* restoration, mostly confined to the borders and folded areas.

Condition B: Posters have more substantial restoration at folds and borders, and may have *some* restoration in other areas.

Note: Special photography was provided by David Graveen. The catalog was produced by Bruce Hershenson, Sylvia Hershenson, and Courier Graphics.

Years of Origin and Studios Listed

The dates listed for Cinema Posters are the date on the posters. In cases where the film was released at the beginning or end of the year, this date may vary from the usually accepted year of release.

The studio is the original releasing studio as indicated on the poster. If no releasing studio is given, the production studio is listed.

AFTER THE AUCTION

Payment
Under normal circumstances, you are expected to pay for your purchases within seven calendar days of the sale and to remove the property you have bought by that date. Payment can be made by check, cash, money order or bank wire transfer. To avoid any delivery delays, prospective buyers are encouraged to supply bank or other suitable references before the auction.

Shipping
After payment has been made in full, Christie's may, as a service to buyers, arrange to have property packed, insured and shipped at your request and expense. For your convenience, a shipping form is enclosed with your invoice and is also available through our Art Transport Department at (212) 606 0455. In circumstances in which Christie's arranges and bills for such services via invoice or credit card, we will also include an administration charge.

We recommend that you request an estimate for any large items or property of high value requiring specialized professional packers.

Sale Results
Price lists are sent automatically to catalogue subscribers and absentee bidders shortly after each sale and are available to others on request. The price list will not include lots that were withdrawn or failed to sell. The price paid for any bought-in lot sold within 24 hours of the auction may be included on the list of prices realized but will be marked to indicate that such price was not realized at the auction. In addition, interested clients can obtain sale results for specific lots during and after the auction by calling (212) 546 1199, Christie's Sale Results Line.

THE SELLER

Auction Estimates

If you are considering selling your property, Christie's is happy to provide a free verbal estimate of its auction value. You can bring items into our New York salerooms at Park Avenue or Christie's East any time during normal business hours. To ensure meeting with the specialist we encourage you to make an appointment in advance with the department. If a visit is not practical, please send a clear photograph together with dimensions and any other pertinent information that you may have.

Estate Services

Christie's Estates and Appraisals Department works closely with lawyers, bankers and others with responsibility for dispersing estates. Please call (212) 546 1060 for information about Christie's extensive estate services.

Consignment Agreement

If you decide to sell your property at auction, the procedures are simple and you should find Christie's specialists and administrative staff helpful to you throughout the process. After discussions with our specialists, you will receive a contract to sign, setting forth terms and fees for services we can provide, such as insurance, shipping and catalogue illustration. For all categories other than stamps, Christie's standard consignor commission rates are 10% of the final bid price on items selling for $7,500 and above, 15% on property selling for $2,000 to $7,499 and 20% for lots bringing less than $2,000. Christie's generally charges a minimum commission of $100 for each lot sold. For stamps, the standard commission rates are 10% of the final bid price on property selling for $2,000 and above and 15% on property selling for less than $2,000, and there is no minimum commission on sold lots. Christie's specialists will discuss with you a suggested reserve price and our recommendations for pre-sale estimates for each piece of property you consign for sale.

Delivery of Property to Christie's

After you have consigned property to us for sale, you can either bring your property to Christie's yourself, arrange with your own shipper to deliver it to us or Christie's specialist department can organize for it to be shipped through Christie's Art Transport Department. We are always happy to assist you. For more information please contact us at (212) 606 0455. Property usually arrives at Christie's at least three months before the sale in order to allow our specialists time to research, catalogue and photograph the items. Prior to the auction your property is generally stored without charge at one of Christie's secure warehouses.

Pre-Auction Notification

Several weeks before the scheduled sale, along with thousands of Christie's worldwide subscribers, you will receive a copy of the sale catalogue in which your property is offered. You will also find enclosed with your catalogue a form indicating your property's lot numbers and confirming the reserves.

Post-Auction Notification

Within a few days after the sale, you will receive a post-sale advice listing the final bid price or, in the event that the property failed to sell, notification that it was bought-in to be returned to you. At any time during or after an auction, you can obtain the selling price for any lot by calling (212) 546 1199.

Approximately 35 days after the sale, pending payment by the purchaser, you will be sent payment for your sold property and a settlement statement itemizing the selling commission and other charges.

CONDITIONS OF SALE

THE PROPERTY DESCRIBED IN THIS CATALOGUE, WHICH DESCRIPTION MAY BE AMENDED BY SALEROOM NOTICE OR ANNOUNCEMENT, WILL BE OFFERED FOR SALE BY CHRISTIE'S ON BEHALF OF VARIOUS CONSIGNORS ("SELLERS"). UNLESS OTHERWISE INDICATED IN THE CATALOGUE, ALL PROPERTY WILL BE OFFERED BY CHRISTIE'S AS AGENT FOR THE SELLER. THESE **CONDITIONS OF SALE** AND THE **LIMITED WARRANTY** SET FORTH ON THE FOLLOWING PAGE, TOGETHER WITH ANY GLOSSARY CONTAINED HEREIN, CONSTITUTE THE COMPLETE AND EXCLUSIVE STATEMENT OF THE TERMS AND CONDITIONS ON WHICH ALL PROPERTY DESCRIBED IN THIS CATALOGUE IS OFFERED FOR SALE, AND THERE ARE NO WARRANTIES, EXPRESS OR IMPLIED, WHICH EXTEND BEYOND THOSE CONTAINED IN SUCH TEXTS. CHRISTIE'S RESERVES THE RIGHT TO VARY THE TERMS OF SALE AND ANY SUCH VARIANCE SHALL BECOME PART OF THESE **CONDITIONS OF SALE**. BY BIDDING AT AUCTION, WHETHER PRESENT IN PERSON OR BY AGENT, BY WRITTEN BID, TELEPHONE OR OTHER MEANS, THE BUYER AGREES TO BE BOUND BY THESE **CONDITIONS OF SALE**.

1. As used in these **Conditions of Sale**, the term "final bid price" means the amount of the highest bid acknowledged by the auctioneer and the term "purchase price" means the sum of the final bid price plus the premium payable by the buyer, as set forth in Condition 4.

2. The highest bidder acknowledged by the auctioneer shall be the buyer. The auctioneer has the right to reject any bid, to advance the bidding at his absolute discretion and, in the event of any dispute between bidders or any other issue with respect to the highest bidder, to determine the successful bidder, to continue the bidding or to reoffer and resell the lot in question. In the event of any dispute after the sale, Christie's record of final sale shall be conclusive.

3. Christie's reserves the right to withdraw any lot before or at the sale.

4. The purchase price payable by a buyer shall be the sum of the final bid price plus a premium of 15% of the final bid price up to and including $50,000 and 10% of the final bid price above $50,000.

5. All lots marked with • next to the lot number are offered subject to a reserve, which is the confidential minimum price below which the lot will not be sold (the "reserve"). Christie's shall act to protect the reserve by bidding through the auctioneer. The auctioneer may open bidding on any lot below the reserve by placing a bid on behalf of the seller. The auctioneer may continue to bid on behalf of the seller up to the amount of the reserve, either by placing consecutive bids or by placing bids in response to other bidders.

6. Title to the offered lot shall pass to the buyer upon the fall of the auctioneer's hammer and announcement by the auctioneer that the lot has been sold, subject to compliance by the buyer with all other **Conditions of Sale**. The buyer shall forthwith assume full risk and responsibility for the lot and shall pay the full purchase price or such part thereof as Christie's, in our sole discretion, shall require. In addition, the buyer may be required to sign a confirmation of purchase.

7. No lot may be removed from Christie's premises until the buyer has paid in full the purchase price therefor or has satisfied such terms as Christie's, in our sole discretion, shall require. Subject to the foregoing, all lots are to be paid for and removed from Christie's premises at the buyer's expense no later than 4:30 p.m. of the seventh calendar day following the sale, and, if not so removed, Christie's may transfer any such lot to a public warehouse for the account, and at the risk and expense of the buyer. The buyer of any lot which remains on Christie's premises later than 4:30 p.m. of the seventh calendar day following the sale will incur a charge for storage and handling of $10.00 per day for each lot. In addition to other remedies available by law, Christie's reserves the right to impose a late charge of 1½% per month on the purchase price commencing on the day following the date on which payment is due if the buyer does not make payment in full in accordance with these **Conditions of Sale**.

8. Bids which are submitted to Christie's in writing or are otherwise left with Christie's prior to an auction for execution at or below a specified price ("absentee bids"), as well as telephone bids, shall be entertained and executed by Christie's for the convenience of bidders not present at auction, but Christie's shall not be responsible for failing to execute such bids or for errors relating to our execution of such bids.

9. Unless exempted by law, the buyer shall be required to pay any applicable state and local sales tax or compensating use tax on the purchase price.

10. If the buyer fails to comply with any of these **Conditions of Sale**, Christie's may, in addition to asserting all remedies available by law, including the right to hold such defaulting buyer liable for the purchase price, (i) cancel the sale, retaining as liquidated damages any payment made by the buyer, (ii) resell the property without reserve at public auction or privately on seven days' notice to the buyer, (iii) pay the seller an amount equal to the net proceeds payable in respect of the purchase price bid by the original defaulting buyer and then resell the property to a third party without reserve at public auction or privately on seven days' notice to the buyer, or (iv) take such other action as it deems necessary or appropriate. If Christie's resells the property, pursuant to clause (ii) or (iii) above, the original defaulting buyer shall be liable for the payment of any deficiency between the original purchase price and the price obtained upon resale pursuant to clause (ii) or (iii) above and all costs and expenses, including warehousing, the expenses of both sales, reasonable attorneys' fees, commissions, incidental damages and all other charges due hereunder. In the event that such buyer pays a portion of the purchase price for any or all lots purchased, Christie's shall apply the payment received to such lot or lots that Christie's, in our sole discretion, deems appropriate. Any buyer who fails to comply with these **Conditions of Sale** will be deemed to have granted Christie's a security interest in, and Christie's may retain as collateral security for such buyer's obligation to Christie's, any property in Christie's possession owned by such buyer. Christie's shall have the benefit of all rights of a secured party under the Uniform Commercial Code adopted in the state where the auction is held.

11. The respective rights and obligations of the parties with respect to the **Conditions of Sale** and the conduct of the auction shall be governed and interpreted by the laws of the state in which the auction is held. By bidding at an auction, whether present in person or by agent, by absentee bid, telephone or other means, the buyer shall be deemed to have consented to the exclusive jurisdiction of the courts of such state and the Federal courts sitting in such state. The buyer expressly agrees that (i) neither Christie's nor the seller shall be liable, in whole or in part, for any special, indirect or consequential damages, including, without limitation, loss of profits and (ii) the buyer's damages are limited exclusively to the original purchase price paid for the lot.

12. Christie's may, in our discretion and as a service to buyers, arrange to have purchased lots packed, insured and forwarded at the request, expense and risk of the buyer. Christie's assumes no responsibility for acts or omissions in such packing or shipping by Christie's or other packers or carriers, whether or not recommended by Christie's. Nor does Christie's assume any responsibility for any damage to picture frames or to the glass therein. In circumstances in which Christie's arranges and bills for such services via invoice or credit card, Christie's will include an administration charge.

LIMITED WARRANTY

Christie's warrants the authenticity of authorship on the terms and conditions and to the extent set forth herein. Subject to the provisions of the last paragraph hereof, Christie's warrants for a period of five years from the date of sale that any property described in headings printed in UPPER CASE TYPE in this catalogue (as such description may be amended by any saleroom notice or announcement) which is unqualifiedly stated to be the work of a named author or authorship, is authentic and not counterfeit. The term "author" or "authorship" refers to the creator of the property or to the period, culture, source or origin, as the case may be, with which the creation of such property is identified in the description of the property in this catalogue. Only UPPER CASE TYPE headings of lots in this catalogue (i.e., headings having capital-letter type) indicate the degree of authenticity of authorship warranted by Christie's. If this catalogue has a glossary, the terms used in such headings are further explained therein. **Any heading which is stated in the Glossary to represent a qualified opinion is not subject to the warranty contained herein. Christie's warranty does not apply to supplemental material which appears below the UPPER CASE TYPE heading of each lot in this catalogue and Christie's is not responsible for any errors or omissions in such supplemental material.**

Christie's warrants to the original buyer of record for a period of twenty-one days from the date of sale that any book or manuscript described in this catalogue is complete in text and illustrations, unless otherwise described. This warranty does not cover binding damages or restoration, stains or foxing, wormholes, short leaves of text or plates or any defect which does not affect the completeness of the text. Nor does this warranty extend to the omission of inserted advertisements, blank leaves, cancels or subsequently published volumes, plate supplements or appendices, atlases, extra-illustrated books, books in original parts, serial publications, items grouped in lots or lots which are described as "sold not subject to return" for any reason whatsoever.

The benefits of this warranty are not assignable and shall be applicable only to the original buyer of the lot and not subsequent assigns, purchasers, heirs, owners or others who have or may acquire an interest therein. This warranty is conditioned upon the buyer returning the lot to Christie's, 502 Park Avenue, New York, N.Y. 10022, in the same condition as at the time of sale.

The buyer's sole and exclusive remedy against Christie's and the seller under this warranty shall be the rescission of the sale and the refund of the original purchase price paid for the lot. This remedy shall be in lieu of any other remedy which might otherwise be available as a matter of law, and neither Christie's nor the seller shall be liable, in whole or in part, for any special, incidental or consequential damages, including, without limitation, loss of profits.

Except as otherwise specifically provided herein, all property is sold "as is" and neither Christie's nor the seller makes any express or implied warranty or representation of any kind or nature with respect to the property. In no event shall Christie's or the seller be responsible for the correctness of, or be deemed to have made, any representation or warranty of merchantability, fitness for purpose, description, size, medium, genuineness, attribution, provenance or condition concerning the property, and no statement set forth in this catalogue or made at the sale or in the bill of sale or invoice or elsewhere, whether oral or written, shall be deemed such a warranty or representation or an assumption of liability. However, the foregoing disclaimer of implied warranties does not apply to articles produced after July 3, 1975. **Christie's and the seller make no warranty or representation, express or implied, that the buyer of any work of art or other property will acquire any copyright or reproduction rights thereto.**

Christie's limited warranty does not apply to the (i) attribution of authorship of paintings, drawings, graphic art or sculpture created before 1870, unless such works are determined to be counterfeit, as such attribution is based on current scholarly opinion, which may change, (ii) attribution of authorship of paintings, drawings,graphic art or sculpture created after 1870 if such attribution at the date of the auction was in accordance with then generally accepted scholarly opinion or fairly indicated there to be a conflict of such opinion or (iii) identification of the period or dates of the execution of any property which may be proven inaccurate by means of a scientific process which was not generally accepted for use until after the date of the auction, unreasonably expensive or impractical to use or likely to have caused damage to the property.

CHRISTIE'S LOS ANGELES SPECIALISTS AND SERVICES

For assistance and further information about this sale, please contact the following:

Specialists In Cinema Posters
Bruce Hershenson, Consultant
Los Angeles
Susan Jensen (310) 275 5534
Catherine Elkies, Director
New York
Andi Allen (212) 606 0543
Timothy Luke, Director

General Information
For 24 hour recorded information:
Current Sales and Exhibitions:
Tel: (212) 371 5438
New York Sales Results
Tel: (212) 546 1199
London Sales Results
King Street Sales (0171) 389 2047/8
South Kensington Sales
(0171) 321 3221
("A" lots are not included)

Catalogue Subscriptions
For information about subscriptions to all our catalogues and publications:
Tel: (800) 395 6300
Fax: (800) 395 5600

Absentee Bids
For arrangement of bids for those who cannot attend the sale:
Terence Ryan
Tel: (310) 275 5534
Fax: (310) 275 9748

Payment
For buyer assistance on terms of payment:
Jeff Baer
Tel: (212) 606 0466
Fax: (212) 737 6076
or method of payment:
Mimi Dowlatshahi
Tel: (310) 275 5534
Fax: (310) 275 9748

Shipping
Professional Packers and Forwarders
3633 Lenawee Avenue
Los Angeles, CA 90016
Tel: (310) 202 6800
Fax: (310) 202 7889

Vendor Settlements
For information on consignor payments:
Elizabeth Mitchell
Tel: (212) 546 1046
Fax: (212) 754 2390

Internet Access
For information about services and forthcoming sales:
http://www.christies.com

Client Services and Telephone Bids
For advice on any aspect of buying in this sale:
Catherine Elkies
Tel: (310) 275 5534
Fax: (310) 275 9748

IMPORTANT NOTICES

Delivery and Collection Information

All Lots will be available for collection during the auction on Sunday December 15th, 1996. Collections will continue at the Pacific Design Center Monday, December 16th between the hours of 9a.m. to 5p.m. On Tuesday December 17th all lots will be transfered to PROFESSIONAL PACKERS & FORWARDERS and will not be available for pick-up.

PP&F is located at 3633 Lenawee Avenue, Los Angeles, CA. Tel: (310) 202 6800
Fax: (310) 202 7889

Collections will resume from PP&F on Wednesday, December 18th through Tuesday, December 31st.

After January 1st, 1997 all storage charges will be at the expense of the purchaser and charged directly by PP&F. For further storage and shipping information please call PP&F directly.

DIRECTIONS TO PACIFIC DESIGN CENTER

We are located at the intersection of San Vicente Blvd. and Melrose Ave. Enter the parking structure at either Melrose Ave. or San Vicente Blvd. Enter at San Vicente Blvd. only after 5 PM, Monday - Friday.

Directions from the following freeways:

1. **Harbor Freeway (11) - Southeast of PDC** (from either direction).
   Harbor Freeway to Santa Monica Freeway (10) West.
   EXIT at La Cienega Blvd North - Proceed 5 miles.
   LEFT at Melrose Ave. - PDC is 3 miles down on the right.

2. **Hollywood Freeway (101) - East of PDC** (from either direction).
   EXIT at Highland Ave. South - Proceed 2 miles.
   RIGHT at Melrose Ave. - PDC is 3 miles down on the right.

3. **Pasadena Freeway (110) - Northeast of PDC.**
   From Pasadena - Pasadena Freeway (110) to Hollywood Freeway (101) North.
   EXIT at Melrose Ave. West - Proceed 5 miles PDC is on the right.

4. **San Diego Freeway (405) - West of PDC** (from either direction).
   EXIT at Santa Monica Blvd. East - Proceed 5 miles.
   RIGHT at San Vicente Blvd. - PDC is 2 blocks down on the left.

5. **Santa Monica Freeway (10) - South of PDC** (from either direction)
   EXIT at La Cienega Blvd. North - Proceed 5 miles.
   LEFT at Melrose Ave. - PDC is 3 blocks down on the right.

6. **Santa Ana Freeway (5) - Southeast of PDC.**
   Santa Ana Freeway North to Santa Monica Freeway (10) West.
   EXIT at La Cienega Blvd. North - Proceed 5 miles.
   LEFT at Melrose Ave. - PDC is 3 blocks down on the right.

7. **Ventura Freeway (134) - Northeast of PDC (Glendale) via Laurel Canyon.**
   Ventura Freeway (134) North becomes Ventura Freeway (101).
   EXIT at Laurel Canyon Ave. South - Proceed 5 miles through the canyon.
   At Sunset Blvd. Laurel Canyon becomes Crescent Heights Blvd. - Proceed 1 mile.
   RIGHT at Melrose Ave. - Proceed 1 mile PDC is on the right.

8. **Ventura Freeway (101) – Northwest of PDC (Encino) via San Diego Freeway**
   East or West of San Diego Freeway - to San Diego Freeway South.
   EXIT at Santa Monica Blvd East - Proceed
   RIGHT at San Vicente Blvd. - PDC is 1 block down on the left.

9. **Ventura Freeway (101) - at North of PDC (Studio City) via Hollywood Freeway.**
   Ventura Freeway South becomes Hollywood Freeway (101) South.
   EXIT at Highland Ave. South - Proceed 2 miles.
   RIGHT at Melrose Ave. - PDC is 3 miles down on the right.

INTRODUCTION

SECTION ONE: ROCK AND POP CINEMA POSTERS

The 173 posters in this section were assembled by a single collector over a fifteen year period. Not only was he attempting to create a comprehensive collection that covered all the different highlights of musical films of the past forty years (with special emphasis on rock and roll), but he also sought out unusual sizes and posters that had extremely limited releases, as well as advance posters that were used prior to a film's release.

This creates a problem in trying to place price estimates on many of the posters in this collection. While there have been hundreds of auctions of regular movie posters, and rock and roll concert posters have been auctioned many times, there has never been a significant sale of posters similar to these. In addition, many of these posters are rarely, if ever, offered for sale privately, and when they are, prices fluctuate wildly.

Therefore, I have attempted to place estimates on the posters that reflect the range I think they might sell in. Of course I realize that several will almost certainly sell for far over the estimates, and as all the posters in this section are being sold without any reserve, several may sell for far under the estimates.

Note that the posters do not have a condition code. This is because all of the posters in this section are in Condition A, except for three posters which are marked Condition B. Non-standard size posters have their dimensions listed under the poster. The dimensions of the standard sizes can be found in the Glossary on page 4.

There are many posters in this section that are extremely rare and unusual, but several deserve to be written about here. The poster for the tenth anniversary release of **The Rocky Horror Picture Show** was withdrawn because of its unauthorized use of Barbie dolls. The Madonna poster for **Dick Tracy** was pulled from release because it was deemed too racy by Disney. The **Captain Eo** poster was only used in the few theme parks where the film was played.

While it is difficult to set price estimates on these posters, it is easy to recognize that this is an extraordinary collection of posters, presenting a visual history of popular music in film over the past forty years.

SECTION TWO: CLASSIC CINEMA POSTERS

This is Christie's ninth auction of vintage movie posters. Christie's held the very first all-movie poster auction by a major auction house in 1990. In many ways, this is the finest of all the Christie's movie poster auctions. It covers virtually all the highlights of the history of the cinema, ranging from the earliest silent films to the best films of the last several decades. There is a special emphasis on the most collected genres: westerns, horror, and comedy. Posters were chosen not only for the historical significance of the film, but also for the visual beauty of the poster, and many visually spectacular posters can be found in these pages. In many cases, posters are offered for historically important films that have great images as well.

Since that very first Christie's movie poster auction six years ago, there have been literally hundreds of auctions at other auction houses, both large and small. This flood of auctions has caused two problems. The lack of high quality material to sell has caused auctions to repeatedly offer the same posters (often with unrealistic reserves) and to offer heavily restored posters. At this auction, only 15% of the posters are repeats from any of the previous Christie's auctions, and many of the the posters have never been auctioned before. Many of the posters are being sold unrestored, and heavily restored posters have not been included in this sale. All of the posters from the last thirty years are offered with no reserve, the same as the posters in Section One.

If one gets the impression looking through these pages that this a museum quality collection of movie posters, it is because it truly is. If this group of posters were kept together, it would represent one of the best collections of movie posters there is. Undoubtedly many of these posters will not be offered again for many years, if ever. This auction represents a once-in-a-lifetime opportunity to purchase some of the finest movie posters known to exist.

-Bruce Hershenson

301 **HAIL! HAIL! ROCK 'N' ROLL**, 1987, one-sheet $100-200

302 **KEEP ON ROCKIN'**
British quad $300-500

303 **HAIL! HAIL! ROCK 'N' ROLL**, 1987, eight lobby cards (two pictured) $100-200

304 **ROCK AROUND THE CLOCK**, 1956, eight lobby cards (two pictured) $500-700

305 **DON'T KNOCK THE ROCK**, 1957, one-sheet $600-800

306 **ROCK 'N' ROLL REVUE,** 1955,
eight lobby cards (one pictured) $700-900

307 **GUYS AND DOLLS,** 1955,
one-sheet $500-700

308 **THE NAT "KING" COLE MUSICAL STORY,** 1955, one-sheet $500-700

309 **DON'T KNOCK THE ROCK,** 1957,
eight lobby cards (two pictured) $300-500

310 **HIGH SOCIETY,** 1956,
one-sheet $500-700

It is interesting to note that **Hey, Let's Twist** featured a very young Joe Pesci, both in the film and on the poster.

311 **TWIST AROUND THE CLOCK,** 1961, three-sheet $300-500

312 **DON'T KNOCK THE TWIST,** 1962, one-sheet $200-400

313 **SCREEN SONG,** 1948, one-sheet $200-300

314 **HEY, LET'S TWIST!,** 1961, six-sheet $1,000-1,500

315 **T.A.M.I. SHOW,** 1964,
one-sheet $300-500

316 **THE BIG T.N.T. SHOW,** 1966,
one-sheet $300-500

318 **IT'S YOUR THING,** 1970,
one-sheet $300-500

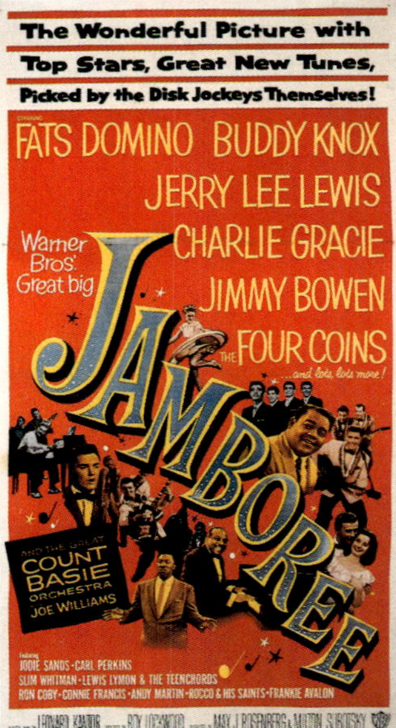

317 **JAMBOREE,** 1957,
three-sheet $400-600

319 **ROCK BABY ROCK IT,** 1957,
one-sheet $400-600

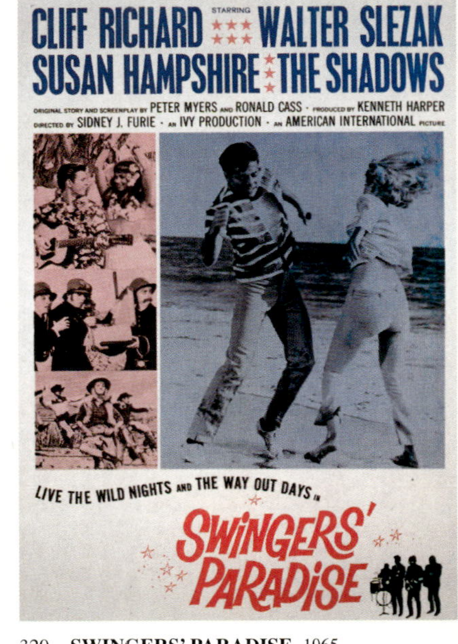

320 **SWINGERS' PARADISE,** 1965,
one-sheet $200-400

321 **THE GIRLS ON THE BEACH,** 1965,
one-sheet $200-300

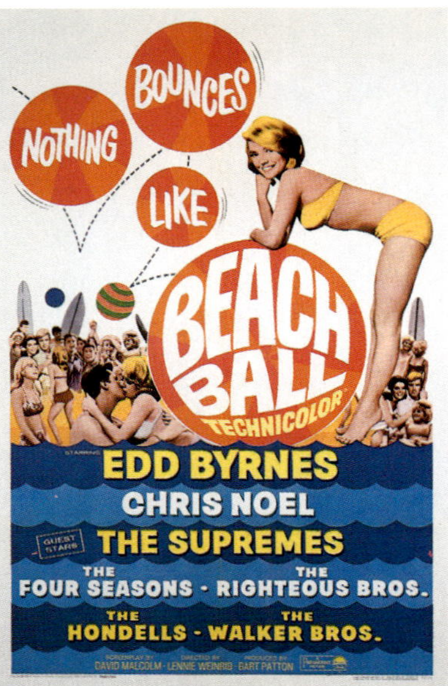

322 **BEACH BALL,** 1965,
one-sheet $200-300

323 **BEACH BLANKET BINGO,** 1965,
one-sheet $300-500

324 **BACK TO THE BEACH,** 1987,
one-sheet $100-200

325 **THE DAVE CLARK FIVE,** 1964,
one-sheet $500-700

326 **GET YOURSELF A COLLEGE GIRL,** 1964,
one-sheet $400-600

327 **WHEN THE BOYS MEET THE GIRLS,** 1965, one-sheet $200-300

328 **CATCH US IF YOU CAN,** 1965, British quad $500-700

329 **MRS. BROWN, YOU'VE GOT A LOVELY DAUGHTER,** 1968, British quad $600-800

330 **C'MON, LET'S LIVE A LITTLE,** 1966, one-sheet $200-400

331 **LOVE AND KISSES,** 1965, one-sheet $300-500

332 **HOUND-DOG MAN,** 1959, one-sheet $300-500

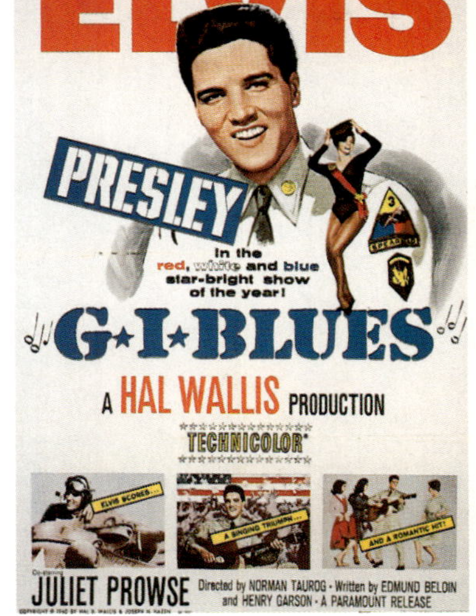

333 **G.I. BLUES,** 1960, one-sheet $400-600

Elvis Presley had a long distinguished film career. Unfortunately, many of his films had undistinguished posters. There were a few happy exceptions, however, and the six Elvis posters offered here are among the very finest that were produced, including a very rare twenty-four sheet (billboard) poster from **Girls! Girls! Girls!** Very few twenty-four sheets are known from any of Elvis' films.

334 **JAILHOUSE ROCK,** 1957,
three-sheet $1,500-2,000

335 **GIRLS! GIRLS! GIRLS!,** 1962,
twenty-four sheet (106 x 234 in) $2,000-3,000

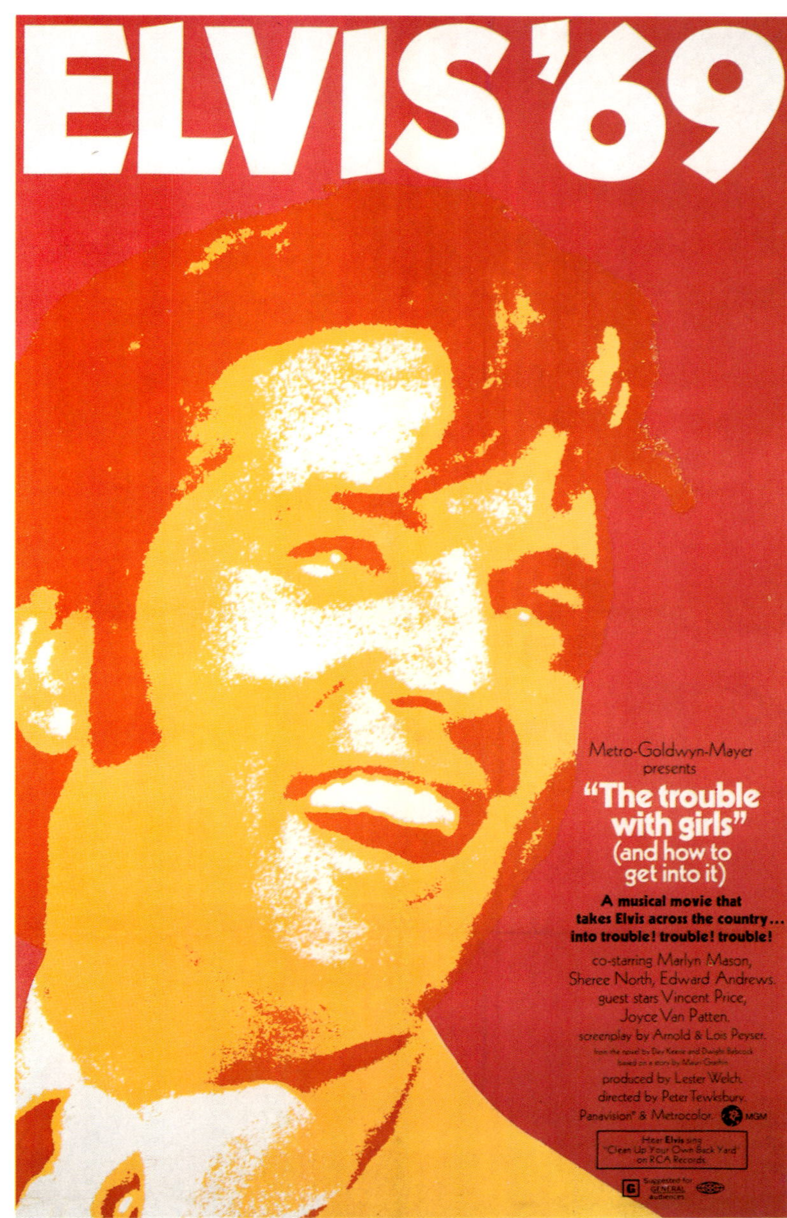

336 **THE TROUBLE WITH GIRLS,** 1969,
one-sheet $300-500

337 **VIVA LAS VEGAS,** 1964,
forty by sixty $1,000-1,500

338 **ELVIS ON TOUR,** 1972,
three-sheet $500-700

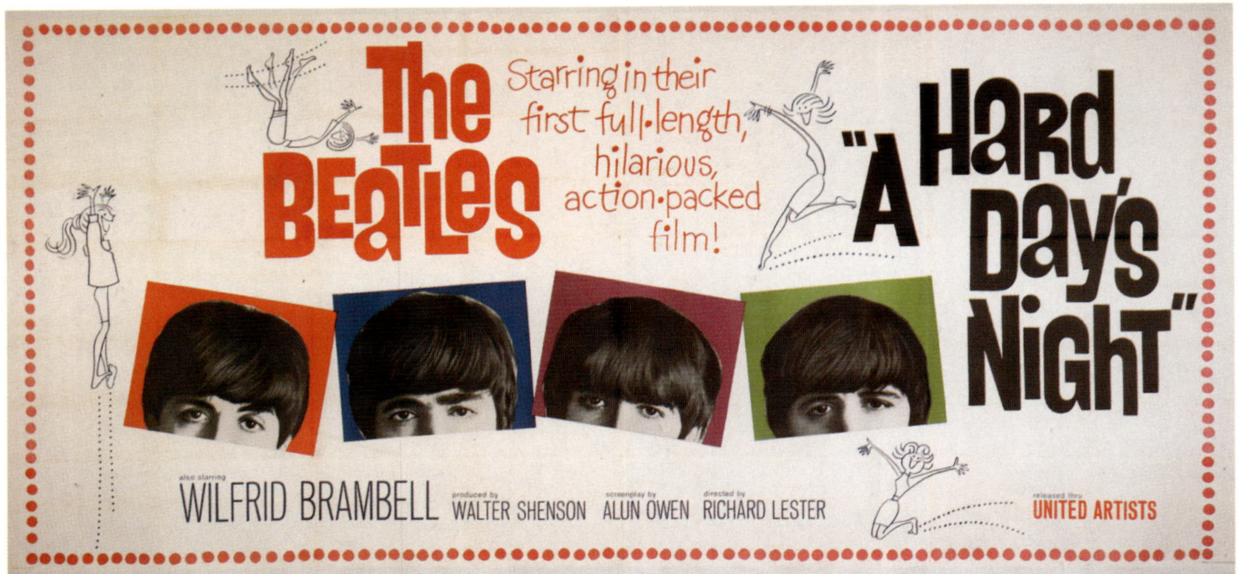

339 **A HARD DAY'S NIGHT,** 1964,
twenty-four sheet (106 x 234 in) $2,000-3,000

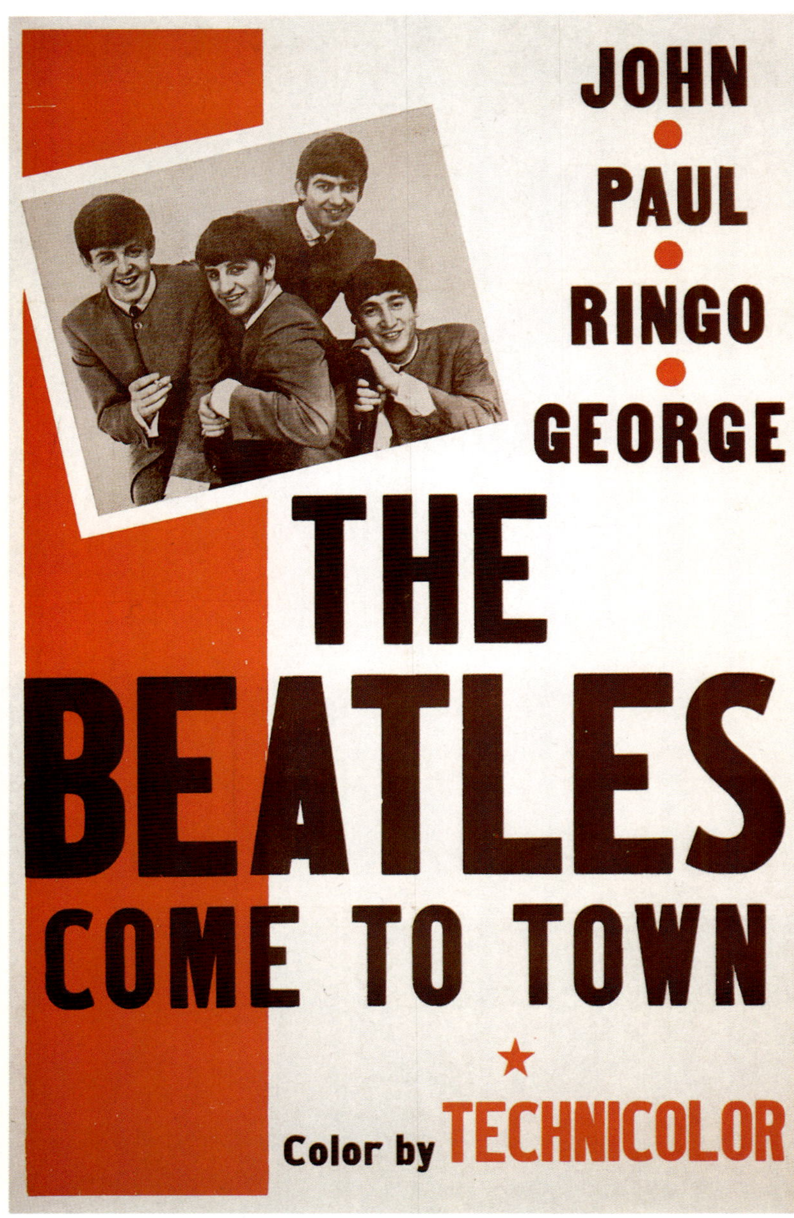

340 **THE BEATLES COME TO TOWN,** 1963,
one-sheet $1,500-2,000

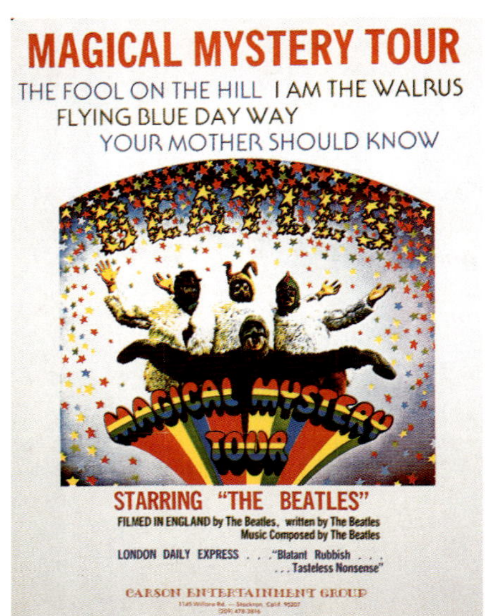

341 **MAGICAL MYSTERY TOUR,** 1967,
special poster (29 x 23 in) $1,000-1,500

342 **YELLOW SUBMARINE,** 1968,
forty by sixty $1,500-2,000

The Beatles Come to Town was a United Artists short that introduced The Beatles to American audiences. **Magical Mystery Tour** was a film that only received a limited 16 mm arthouse release.

The British quad for **A Hard Day's Night** is from a specific theater in England at which the film played.

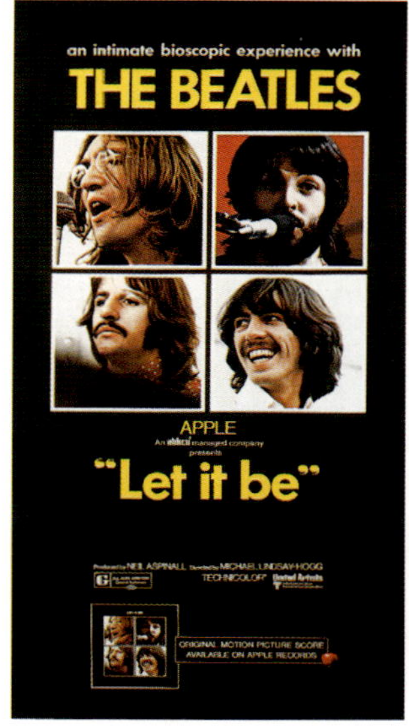

343 **LET IT BE,** 1970, three-sheet $1,000-1,500

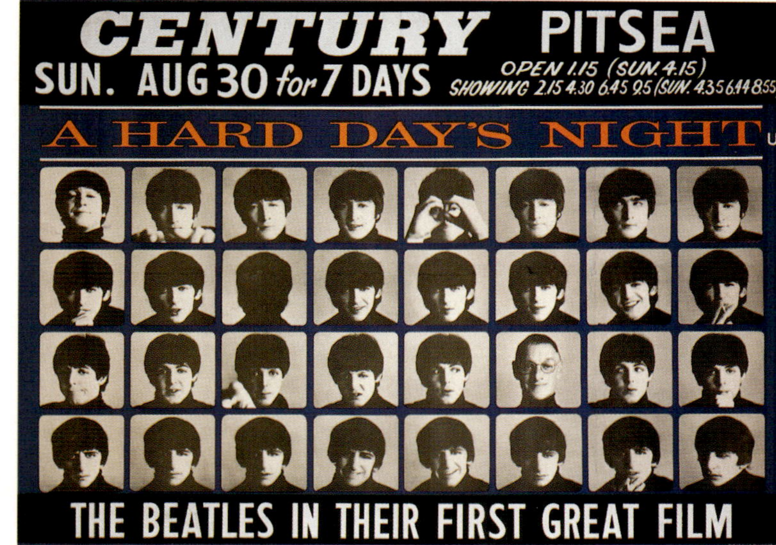

344 **A HARD DAY'S NIGHT,** 1964, British quad $1,000-1,500

345 **HELP,** 1965, six-sheet $1,500-2,000

346 **ROCKSHOW,** 1979,
one-sheet $200-400

347 **GET BACK,** 1991,
one-sheet $200-400

348 **IMAGINE: JOHN LENNON,** 1988,
one-sheet $200-300

349 **RAGA,** 1971,
special poster (30 x 20 in) $300-500

Offered here is the only known copy of **Films by John Lennon & Yoko Ono**.

350 **FILMS BY JOHN LENNON & YOKO ONO,** 1980, special poster (39 x 27 in) $2,000-3,000

351 **SYMPATHY FOR THE DEVIL,** 1968,
French poster $1,500-2,000

352 **PERFORMANCE,** 1970,
subway poster (45 x 60 in) $600-800

353 **GIMME SHELTER,** 1970,
one-sheet $400-600

354 **LET'S SPEND THE NIGHT TOGETHER,**
1982, forty by sixty $400-600

355 **LET'S SPEND THE NIGHT TOGETHER,** 1982,
eight lobby cards (two pictured) $200-400

356 **DANCING IN THE STREET,** 1987, one-sheet $300-500

357 **ZIGGY STARDUST,** 1983, one-sheet $200-400

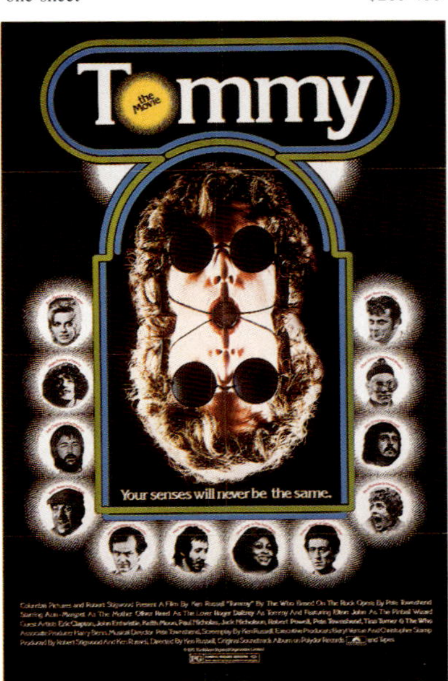

358 **TOMMY,** 1975, one-sheet $300-500

359 **THE KIDS ARE ALRIGHT,** 1979, special poster (39 x 25 in) $400-600

360 **LISZTOMANIA,** 1975, British quad (Cond. B) $300-500

361 **HEAD,** 1968,
one-sheet $500-700

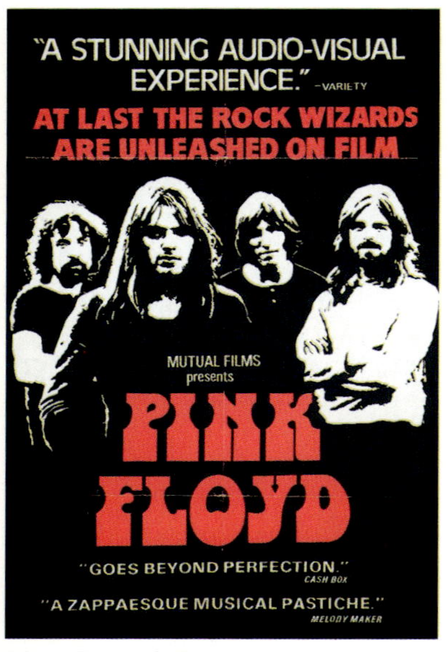

362 **PINK FLOYD,** 1973,
one-sheet $400-600

364 **THE WALL,** 1982,
special poster (67 x 42 in) $600-800

363 **THE VALLEY OBSCURED BY CLOUDS,** 1972,
British quad $400-600

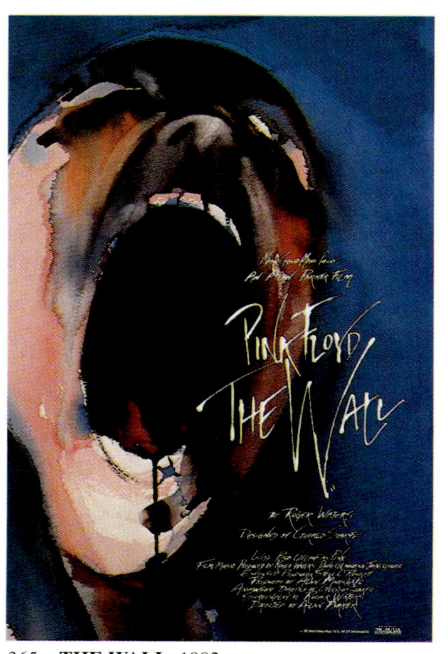

365 **THE WALL,** 1982,
one-sheet $200-400

366 **JIMI PLAYS BERKELEY,** 1971,
display (34 x 44 in) $800-1,200

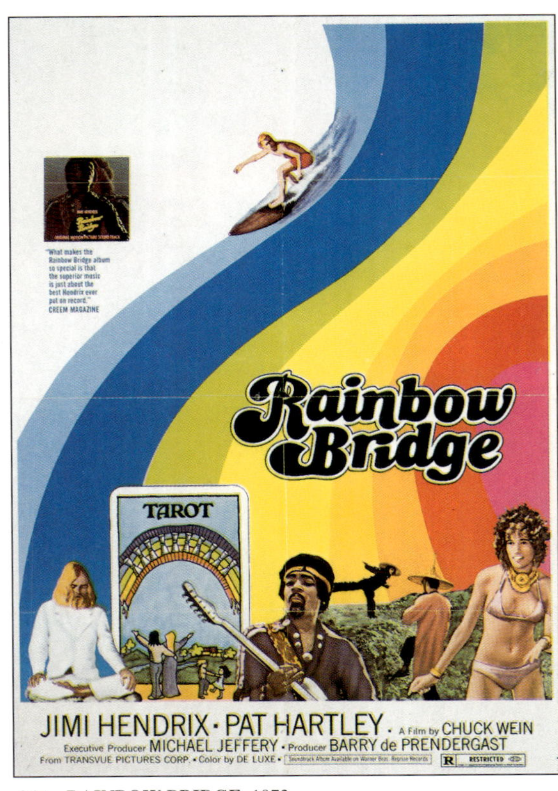

367 **RAINBOW BRIDGE,** 1972,
one-sheet $300-500

368 **A FILM ABOUT JIMI HENDRIX,** 1973,
one-sheet $400-600

369 **JANIS,** 1975,
forty by sixty $500-700

370 **MAD DOGS & ENGLISHMEN,** 1971,
one-sheet (Cond. B) $400-600

371 **THE GRATEFUL DEAD,** 1977,
half-sheet (28 x 22 in) $400-600

372 **200 MOTELS,** 1971,
thirty by forty $600-800

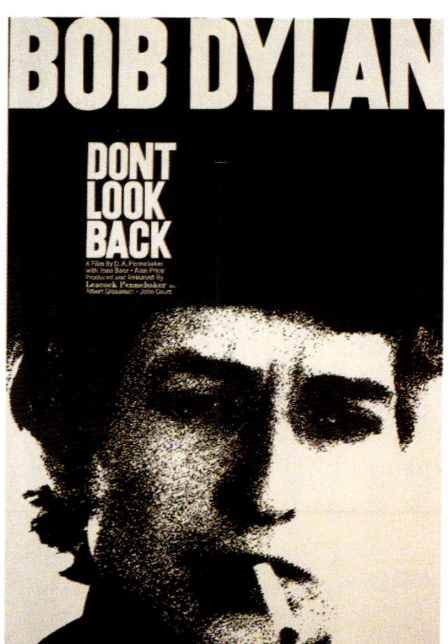

373 **DON'T LOOK BACK,** 1967,
one-sheet $600-800

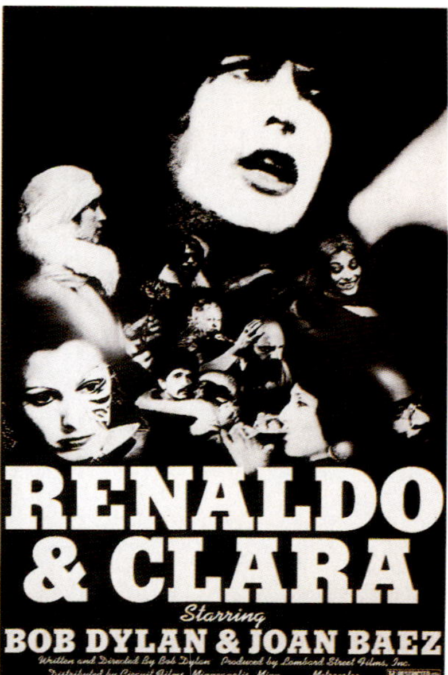

374 **RENALDO & CLARA,** 1978,
one-sheet $600-800

375 **DON'T LOOK BACK,** 1967,
British Crown (30 x 20 in) $600-800

376 **THE CONCERT FOR BANGLADESH,**
1972, forty by sixty $400-600

377 **SAVE THE CHILDREN,** 1973,
one-sheet $300-500

378 **THE CONCERT FOR KAMPUCHEA,**
1981, forty by sixty $400-600

379 **FILLMORE,** 1972,
forty by sixty $400-600

380 **FILLMORE,** 1972,
eight lobby cards (two pictured) $300-500

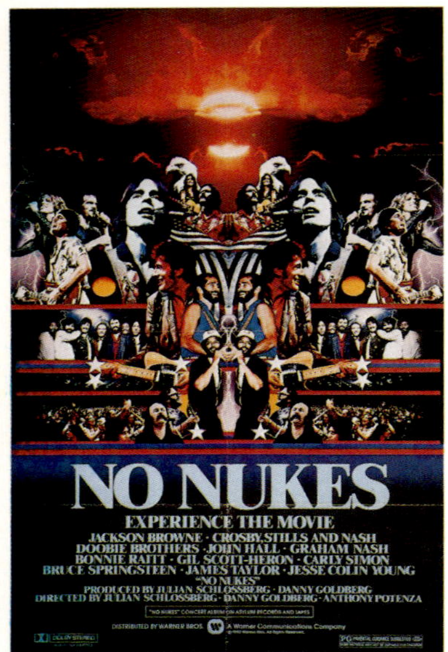

381 **NO NUKES,** 1980, one-sheet $200-400

382 **WOODSTOCK,** 1970, South African one-sheet $400-600

383 **WOODSTOCK,** 1975, reissue, one-sheet $200-400

384 **WOODSTOCK,** 1970, six-sheet $1,500-2,000

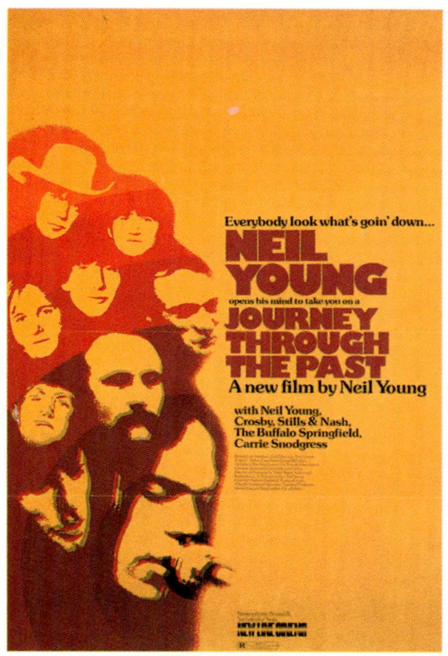

385 **JOURNEY THROUGH THE PAST,** 1974, one-sheet $600-800

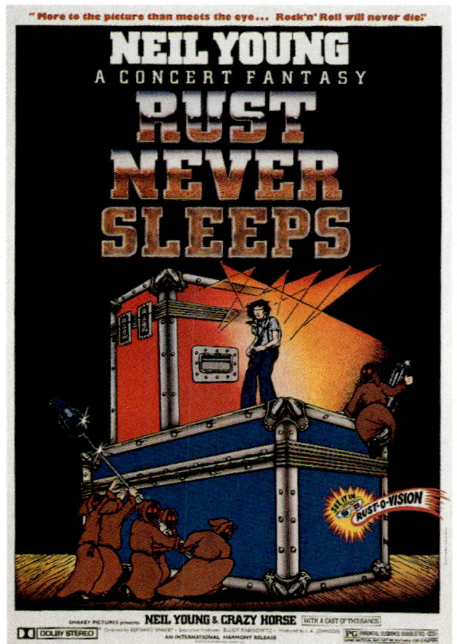

386 **RUST NEVER SLEEPS,** 1979, one-sheet $300-500

388 **MONTEREY POP,** 1969, one-sheet $400-600

387 **RUST NEVER SLEEPS,** 1979, British quad $300-500

389 **YOU ARE WHAT YOU EAT,** 1968, one-sheet $300-500

390 **COUNTRY MUSIC,** 1972,
one-sheet $300-500

391 **TENNESSEE JAMBOREE,** 1964,
one-sheet $300-500

393 **THE FASTEST GUITAR ALIVE,** 1967,
one-sheet $400-600

392 **JOHNNY CASH,** 1969,
one-sheet $400-600

394 **NASHVILLE REBEL,** 1966,
one-sheet $200-400

395 **HAIR,** 1979,
one-sheet $200-400

396 **YESSONGS,** 1975,
one-sheet $400-600

397 **GOOD TIMES,** 1967,
forty by sixty $600-800

398 **TIME WILL TELL,** 1991,
British quad $100-200

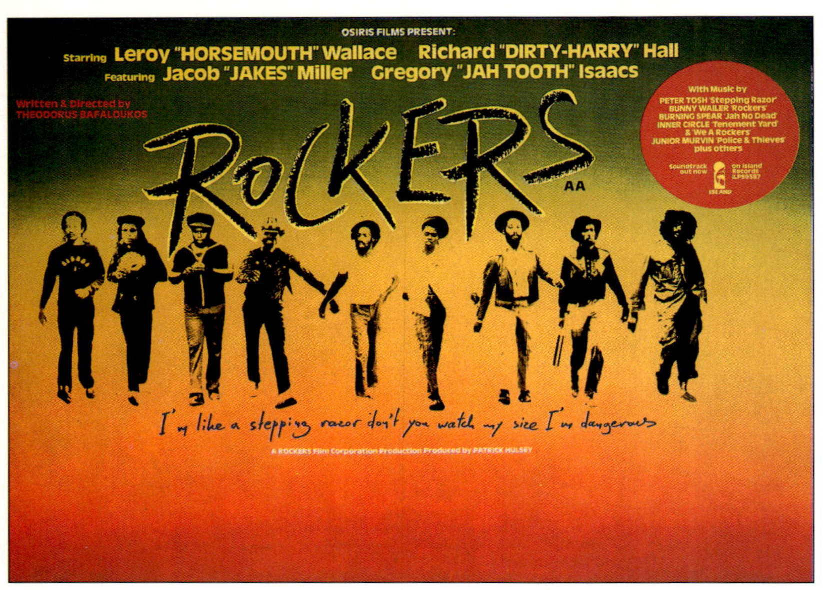

399 **ROCKERS,** 1978,
British quad $300-500

400 **HEAVY METAL,** 1981,
one-sheet $200-400

401 **THE HARDER THEY COME,** 1973,
British quad $400-600

402 **AMERICAN POP,** 1981,
one-sheet $100-200

403 **BRING ON THE NIGHT,** 1985,
one-sheet $200-400

404 **BRING ON THE NIGHT,** 1985,
British quad $300-500

405 **BUGS BUNNY IN CONCERT,** 1990, one-sheet $400-600

406 **THE LION KING,** 1994, half-sheet $200-400

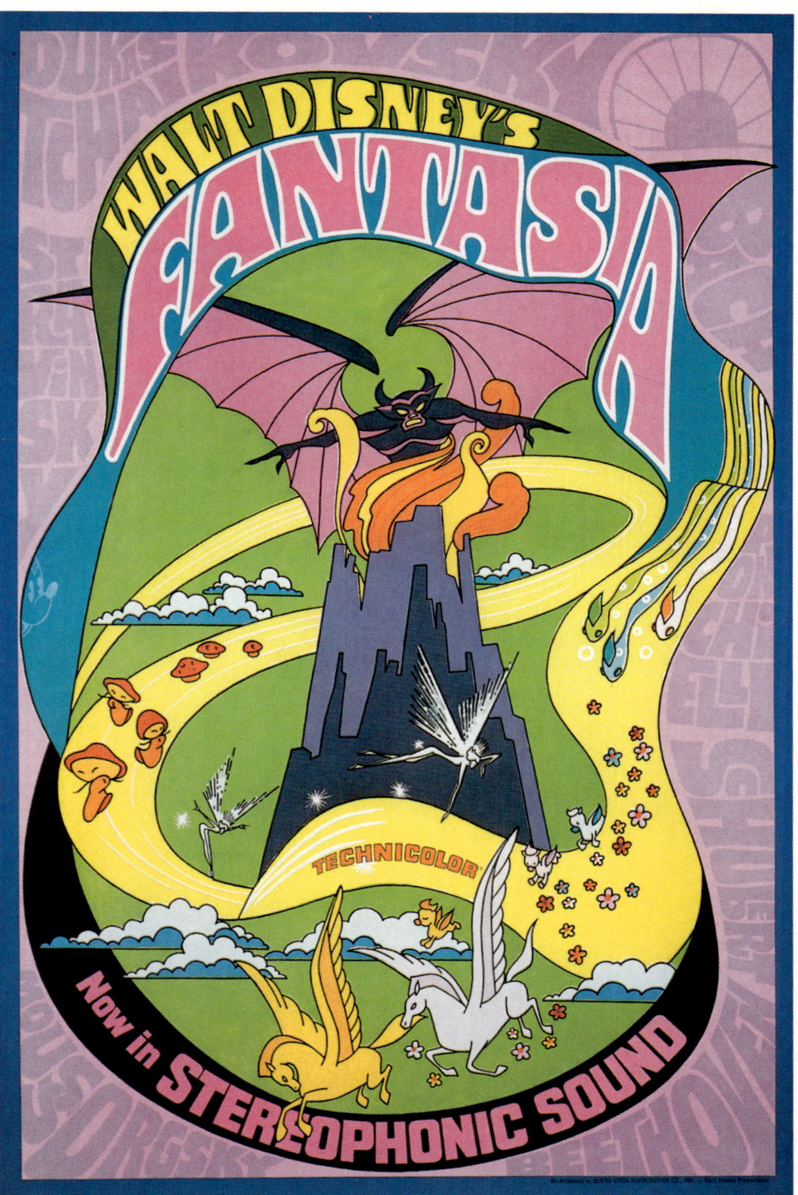

408 **FANTASIA,** 1970 reissue, one-sheet $400-600

407 **BEAUTY AND THE BEAST,** 1992, one-sheet $200-400

409 **SINGIN' IN THE RAIN,** 1952, one-sheet (Cond. B) $1,000-1,500

410 **A STAR IS BORN,** 1954, one-sheet $500-700

411 **THE SOUND OF MUSIC,** 1965,
one-sheet $400-600

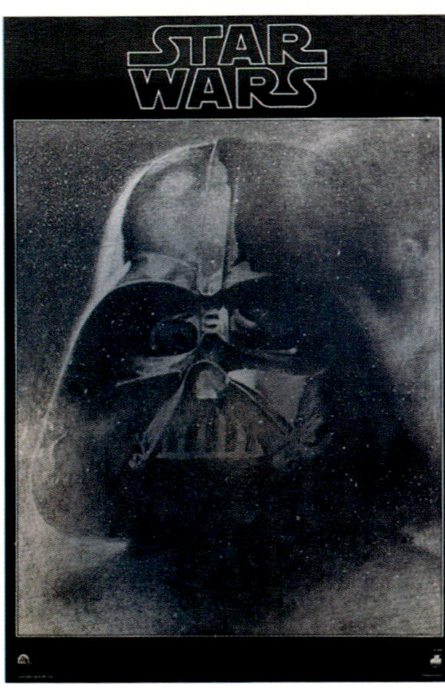

412 **STAR WARS,** 1977,
record promo (33 x 22 in) $400-600

413 **MY FAIR LADY,** 1964,
two door panels (each 60 x 20 in) $600-800

414 **MY FAIR LADY,** 1964,
six-sheet $800-1,200

415 **FUNNY GIRL,** 1968,
forty by sixty $400-600

416 **A STAR IS BORN,** 1976,
forty by sixty $400-600

417 **A STAR IS BORN,** 1976,
concert poster (41 x 27 in) $800-1,200

The concert poster for **A Star is Born** is from an actual concert that Jon Peters organized so that the film could contain authentic footage of Streisand and Kristofferson performing!

418 **HELLO DOLLY,** 1969,
special poster (108 in diameter) $800-1,200

419 **CAN'T STOP THE MUSIC,** 1980,
one-sheet $200-400

The **John Travolta** record promo poster was for an album Travolta recorded while still a cast member of Welcome Back, Kotter.

420 **DISCO FEVER,** 1978,
one-sheet $200-400

421 **SATURDAY NIGHT FEVER,** 1977,
forty by sixty $500-700

422 **GREASE,** 1978,
forty by sixty $500-700

423 **JOHN TRAVOLTA,** 1976,
record promo (22 x 22 in) $400-600

424 **FAME,** 1980,
soundtrack poster (36 x 24 in) $200-400

425 **THE GRADUATE,** 1967,
one-sheet $700-900

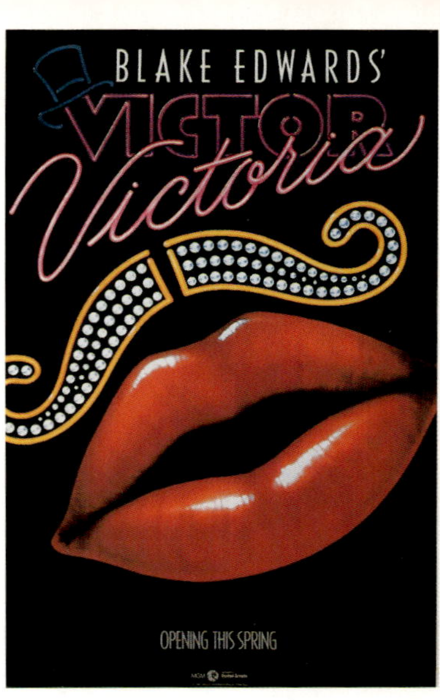

426 **VICTOR, VICTORIA,** 1981,
one-sheet $200-400

427 **CABARET,** 1972,
one-sheet $400-600

428 **NEW YORK, NEW YORK,** 1977,
one-sheet $200-400

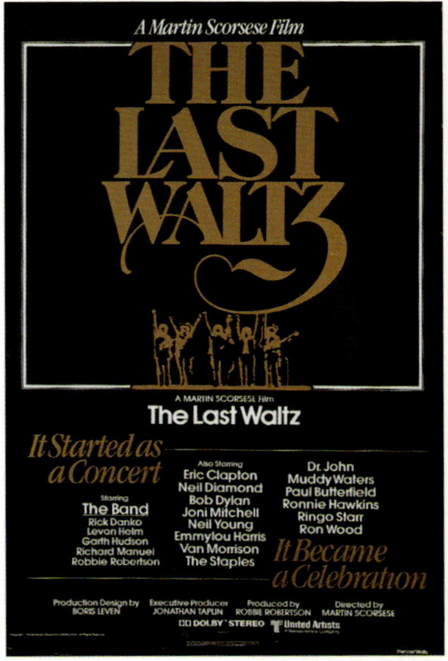

429 **THE LAST WALTZ,** 1978,
one-sheet $300-500

430 **FLASHDANCE,** 1983,
one-sheet $200-400

431 **FOOTLOOSE,** 1984,
one-sheet $200-400

432 **DIRTY DANCING,** 1987,
one-sheet $100-200

433 **THE ROCKY HORROR PICTURE SHOW**, 1975, one-sheet $300-500

434 **THE ROCKY HORROR PICTURE SHOW**, 1985 reissue, one-sheet $500-700

435 **AMERICAN GRAFFITI**, 1973, one-sheet $300-500

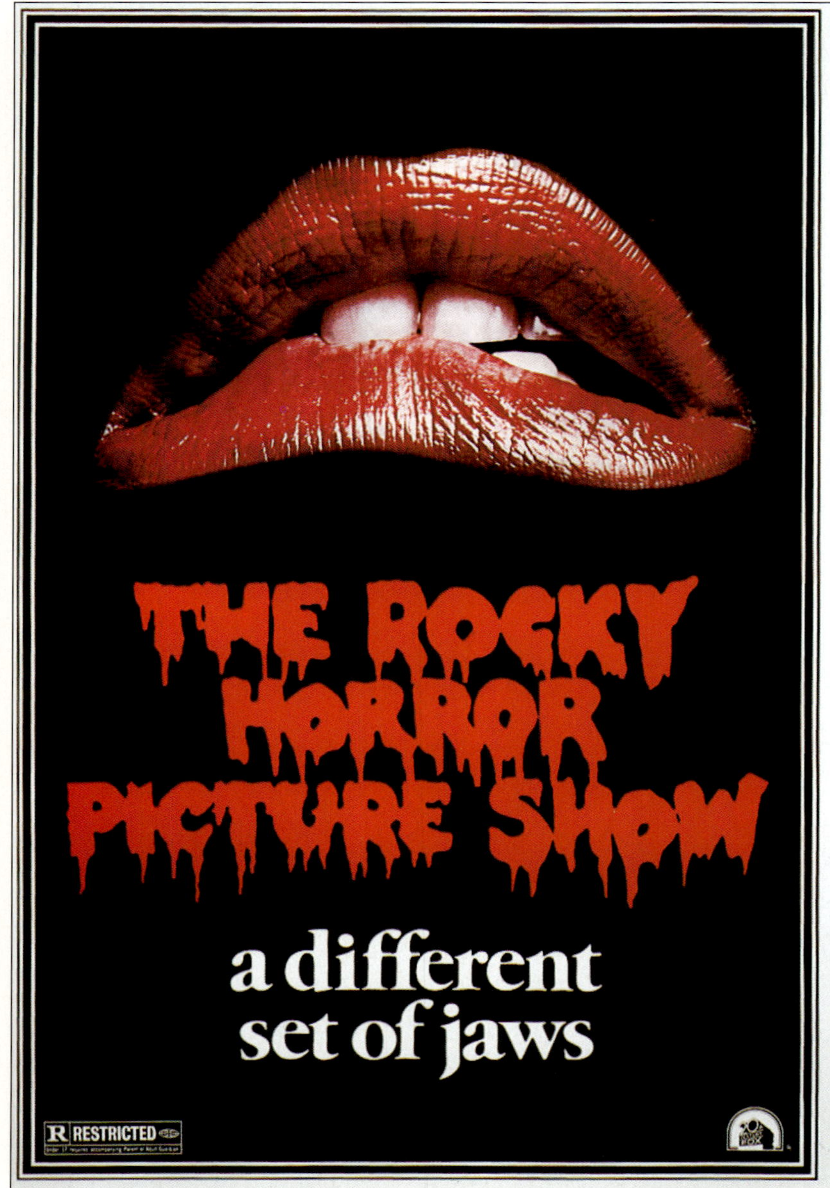

436 **THE ROCKY HORROR PICTURE SHOW**, 1975, one-sheet $300-500

437 **A CHORUS LINE,** 1985, one-sheet $100-200

438 **LISTEN UP,** 1990, one-sheet $100-200

439 **ANIMAL HOUSE**, 1978,
subway poster (45 x 60 in)

$700-900

440 **THE BLUES BROTHERS,** 1980,
subway poster (45 x 60 in)

$700-900

441 **THE LAST OF THE BLUE DEVILS,** 1979, one-sheet $300-500

442 **BLUES UNDER THE SKIN**, 1972, special poster (23 x 16 in) $200-400

443 **BLUES FOR LOVERS,** 1966, one-sheet $400-600

444 **CAPTAIN EO,** 1986, special poster (29 x 19 in) $500-700

445 **LADY SINGS THE BLUES,** 1972, three-sheet $1,000-1,500

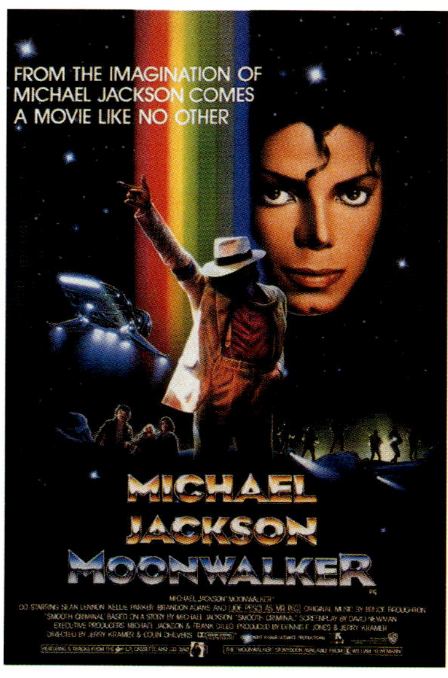

446 **MOON WALKER,** 1988, special poster (30 x 20 in) $200-400

447 **THE WIZ,** 1978,
subway poster (45 x 60 in) $300-500

448 **WE WILL ROCK YOU**
South African one sheet $400-600

449 **PURPLE RAIN**, 1984,
one-sheet $300-500

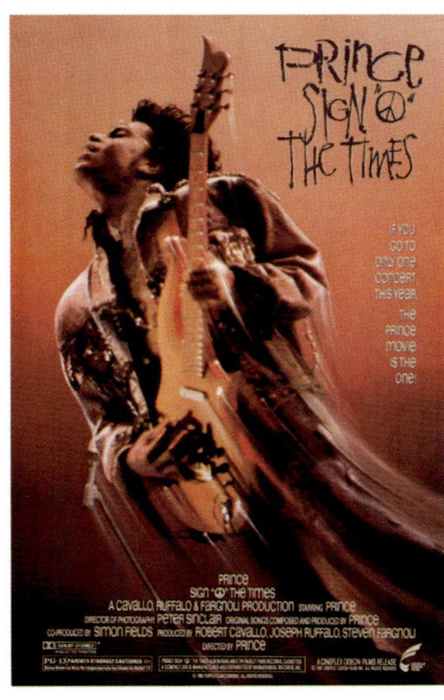

450 **SIGN "☮" THE TIMES,** 1987,
one-sheet $200-400

451 **GRAFFITI BRIDGE,** 1990,
one-sheet $200-400

452 **DESPERATELY SEEKING SUSAN,**
1985, one-sheet $100-200

453 **IN BED WITH MADONNA,** 1991,
one-sheet $200-400

454 **DICK TRACY,** 1990,
one-sheet $300-500

455 **WHITE ROCK,** 1976,
British quad $300-500

456 **JUBILEE,** 1978,
British Crown (30 x 20 in) $300-500

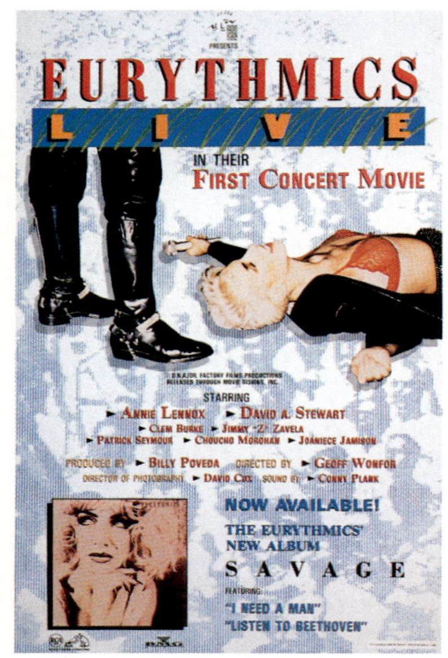

457 **EURYTHMICS LIVE,** 1988,
one-sheet $300-500

458 **DOGS IN SPACE,** 1987,
one-sheet $300-500

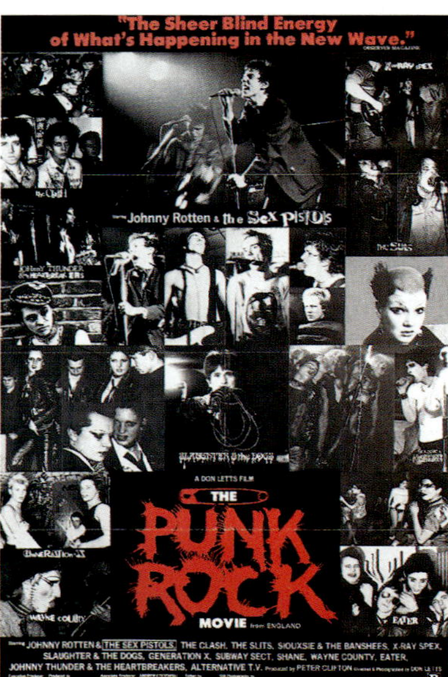

459 **THE PUNK ROCK MOVIE,** 1978,
one-sheet $300-500

460 **THE YEAR PUNK BROKE,** 1992,
one-sheet $300-500

461 **THE CURE IN ORANGE,** 1987,
British quad $400-600

462 **THE GREAT ROCK 'N' ROLL SWINDLE,** 1980, British quad $400-600

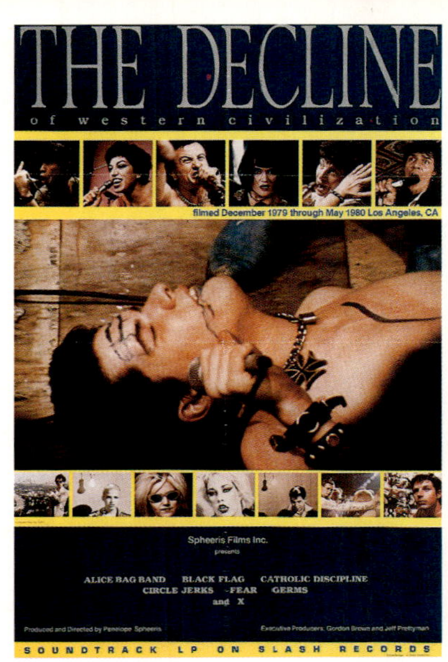

463 **THE DECLINE OF WESTERN CIVILIZATION,** 1981, one-sheet $300-500

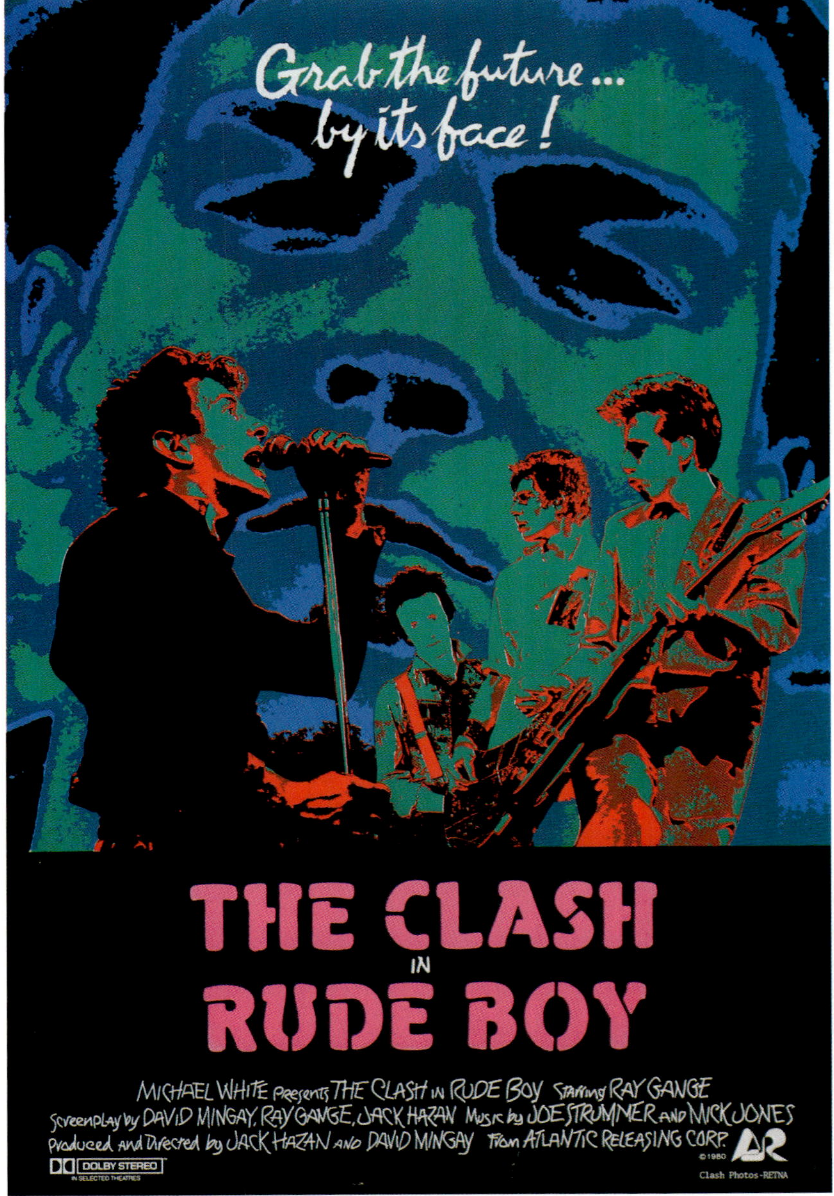

464 **RUDE BOY,** 1980, one-sheet $400-600

465 **KRUSH GROOVE,** 1985, subway poster, (45 x 29 in) $100-200

466 **TOUGHER THAN LEATHER,** 1988, one-sheet $200-400

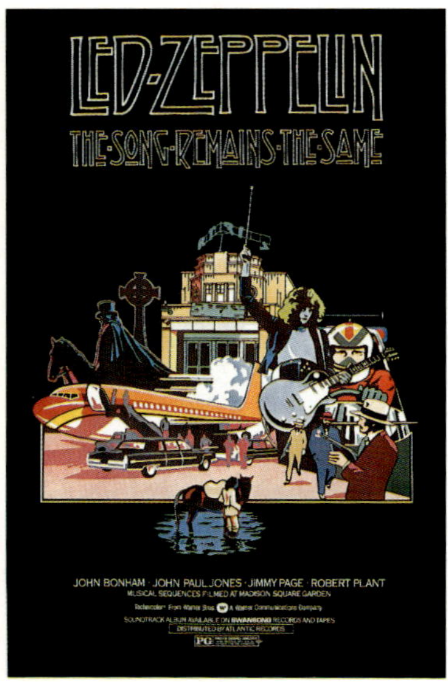

467 **THE SONG REMAINS THE SAME,** 1976, forty by sixty $400-600

468 **ATTACK OF THE PHANTOMS,** 1968, one-sheet $500-700

469 **LET THERE BE ROCK**, 1982, one-sheet $300-500

470 **KILLER KLOWNS,** 1988, soundtrack promo (18 x 24 in)  $400-600

471 **BLACK AND BLUE,** 1980, special poster (35 x 23 in) $300-500

472 **RATTLE AND HUM,** 1988, one-sheet $300-500

Attack of the Phantoms was the only film that Kiss made, and it received limited distribution.

473 **THE BODYGUARD,** 1992, banner (46 x 120 in) $200-400

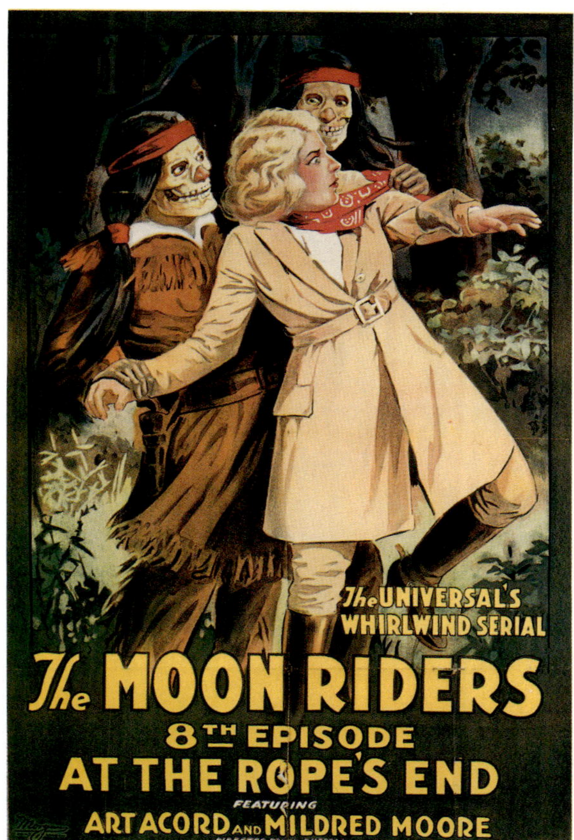

• 501 **THE MOON RIDERS**, Universal, 1920, one-sheet, Cond. B
41 x 27 in $700-900

The cowards never started:—
The weak died on the way.
JESSE L. LASKY Presents a
JAMES CRUZE Production
THE COVERED WAGON
ADAPTED BY JACK CUNNINGHAM
FROM THE NOVEL BY EMERSON HOUGH
a Paramount Picture

• 502 **THE COVERED WAGON**, Paramount, 1923, one-sheet, Cond. A, linen backed
41 x 27 in $2,000-3,000

• 503 **OUTLAWED**, F.B.O., 1929, one-sheet, Cond. A, linen backed
41 x 27 in $1,500-2,000

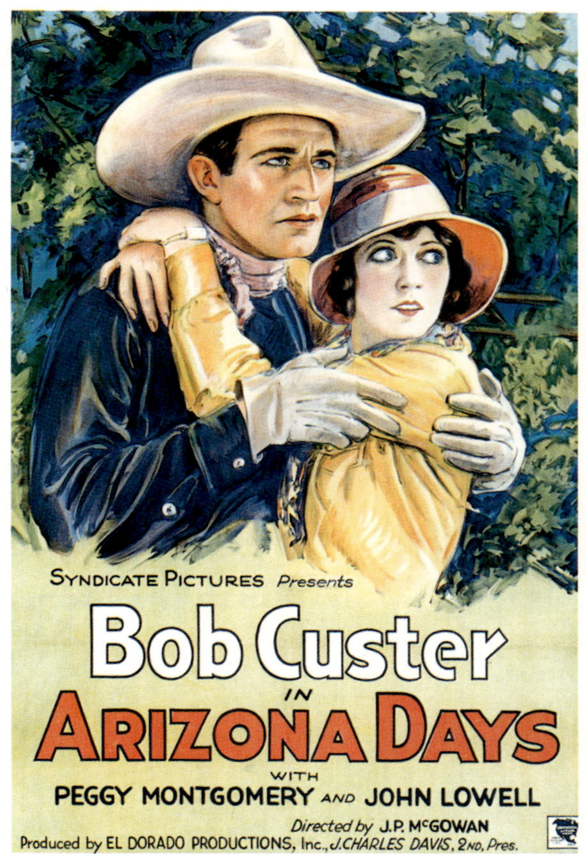

• 504 **ARIZONA DAYS**, Syndicate, 1928, one-sheet, Cond. A, linen backed
41 x 27 in $600-800

• 505 **JESSE JAMES,** Paramount, 1927, one-sheet, Cond. A
41 x 27 in $1,500-2,000

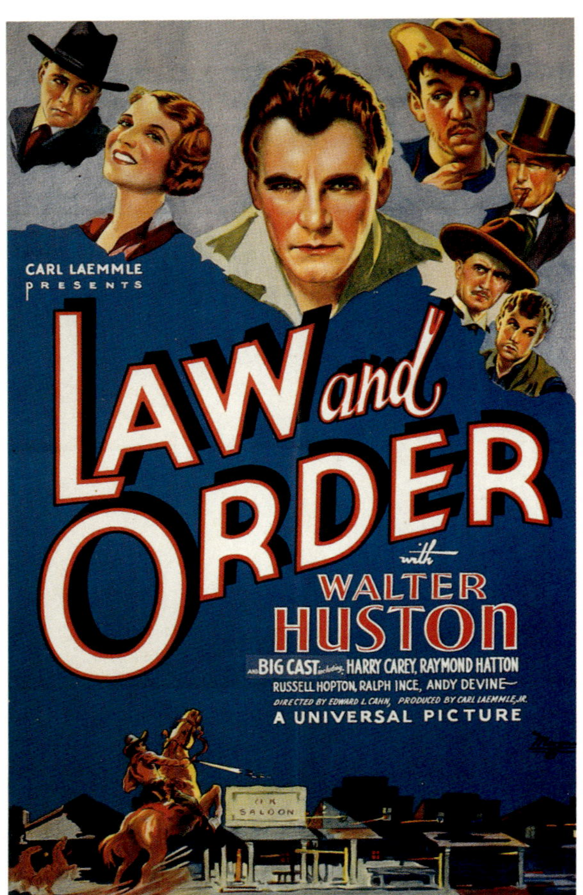

• 506 **LAW AND ORDER,** Universal, 1932, one-sheet, Cond. A
41 x 27 in $1,000-1,500

• 507 **UNDER THE TONTO RIM,** Paramount, 1933, one-sheet, Cond. B, linen backed
41 x 27 in $1,500-2,000

• 508 **THE VIRGINIAN,** Paramount, 1929, insert, Cond. B, linen backed
36 x 14 in $1,500-2,500

The western film was a staple of the silent cinema. In 1929, **The Virginian** was filmed as a silent film, but a sound version was released as well. The very rare "all-talking" style one-sheet is offered here, as well as a striking insert from the silent release.

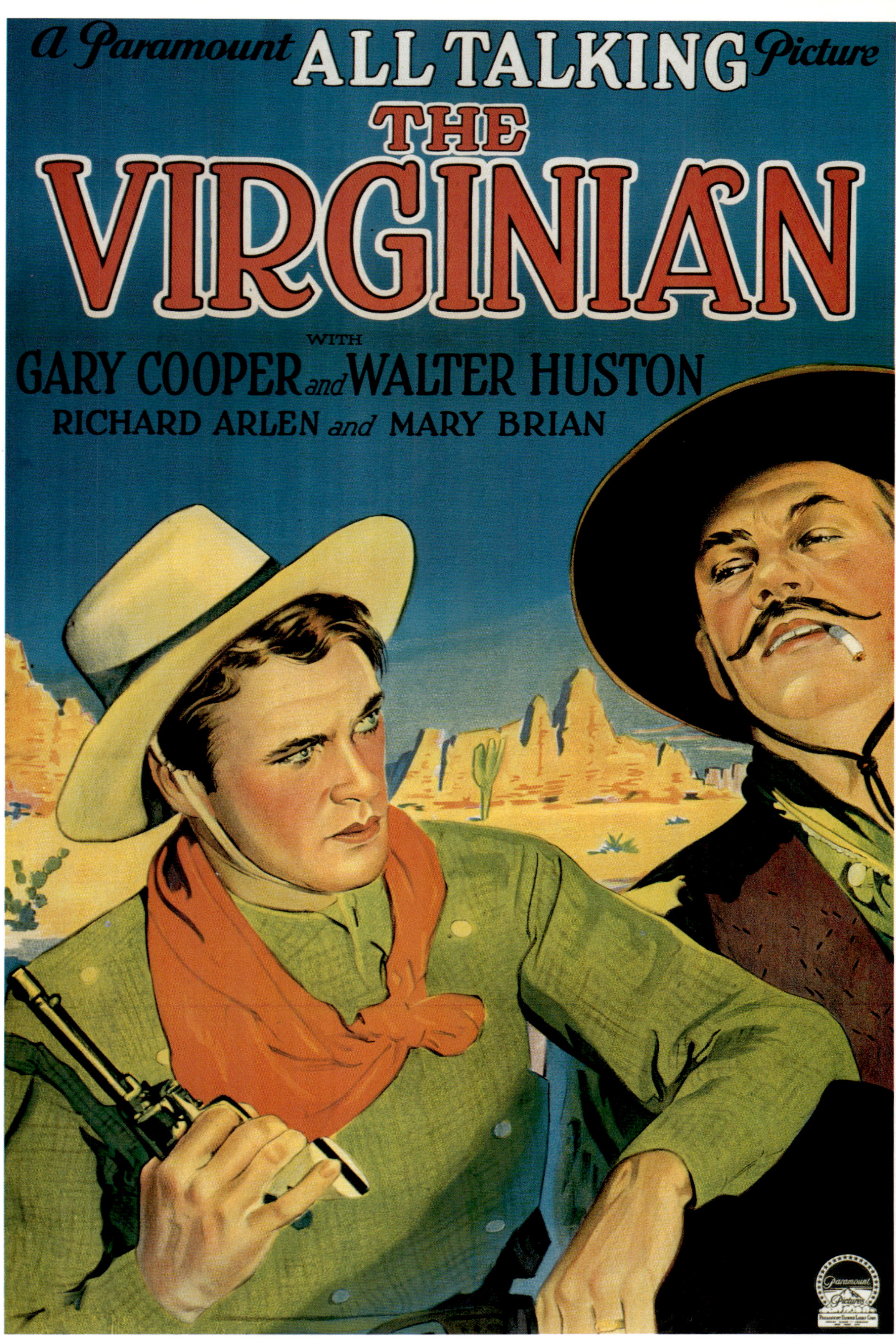

• 509 **THE VIRGINIAN,** Paramount, 1929, one-sheet, Cond. A, linen backed
41 x 27 in $5,000-7,000

By the early 1930s, western films were increasingly relegated to the lower half of the double bill. One studio, Columbia, made beautiful stone lithograph one-sheet posters to promote these B-westerns.

• 510 **SOUTH OF THE RIO GRANDE,** Columbia, 1932, one-sheet, Cond. A, linen backed
41 x 27 in $4,000-6,000

Columbia's top cowboy star was Charles "Buck" Jones. The one-sheet posters for **South of the Rio Grande** and **Ridin' for Justice** are considered by many to be the two finest western film posters ever created.

• 511 **RIDIN' FOR JUSTICE,** Columbia, 1931, one-sheet, Cond. A, linen backed
41 x 27 in $4,000-6,000

Columbia's other top cowboy star was Colonel Tim McCoy. Collectors especially prize posters that show the star in full cowboy garb pointing a gun, and four of the finest are offered here.

• 512 **MAN OF ACTION,** Columbia, 1933, one-sheet, Cond. A, paper backed
41 x 27 in $1,000-1,500

• 513 **CORNERED,** Columbia, 1932, one-sheet, Cond. A, linen backed
41 x 27 in $900-1,200

• 514 **THE DAWN TRAIL,** Columbia, 1930, one-sheet, Cond. A, linen backed
41 x 27 in $900-1,200

• 515 **SILENT MEN,** Columbia, 1933, one-sheet, Cond. A, linen backed
41 x 28 in $900-1,200

The Phantom Empire stands alone among 1930s films. This serial managed to combine cowboys, music, robots, and an underground civilization, as well as future superstar Gene Autry. Single one-sheets from this serial are very rare and highly prized. Offered here are the complete set of lobby cards from Chapter One, as well as **all** the one-sheets from Chapters Two through Twelve, an amazing collection that almost certainly could not be duplicated.

• 516 **THE PHANTOM EMPIRE,** Mascot, 1935,
eleven one-sheets (three pictured) and set of eight lobby cards (two pictured), all Cond. A
41 x 27 in and 11 x 14 in $14,000-18,000

One-sheets from the 1938 serial **The Lone Ranger** are highly prized. Offered here are both the one-sheet for the entire serial as well as a circus poster with a similar image promoting a personal appearance by the actor who portrayed The Lone Ranger.

• 517 **THE LONE RANGER,** Republic, 1938, one-sheet, Cond. A (has glued-on snipe)
41 x 27 in $2,000-3,000

• 518 **THE LONE RANGER,** 1938, special circus poster, Cond. B (has glued-on snipe)
45 x 27 in $1,500-2,000

• 519 **GORDON OF GHOST CITY,** Universal, 1933, one-sheet, Cond. A
41 x 27 in $900-1,200

• 520 **STONE OF SILVER CREEK,** Universal, 1935, one-sheet, Cond. A
41 x 27 in $800-1,000

Buck Jones left Columbia to join Universal Pictures in 1934, and Universal prepared dazzling one-sheets to promote their new star. **Billy the Kid Returns** was the second film appearance of Roy Rogers.

• 521 **THE THROWBACK,** Universal, 1935, one-sheet, Cond. A
41 x 27 in $800-1,000

• 522 **SANDFLOW,** Universal, 1936, one-sheet, Cond. A, linen backed
41 x 27 in $800-1,000

• 523 **WHEN A MAN SEES RED,** Universal, 1934, one-sheet, Cond. A, linen backed
41 x 27 in $900-1,200

• 524 **BILLY THE KID RETURNS,** Republic, 1938, one-sheet, Cond. A, linen backed
41 x 27 in $800-1,000

• 525 **HEART OF THE WEST,** Paramount, 1936, three-sheet, Cond. B, linen backed
81 x 41 in $900-1,200

• 526 **HEART OF THE WEST,** Paramount, 1936, one-sheet, Cond. B, linen backed
41 x 27 in $700-900

• 527 **THE LONELY TRAIL,** Republic, 1936, three-sheet, Cond. B, linen backed
81 x 41 in $4,000-6,000

William Boyd first portrayed Hopalong Cassidy in 1935. **Heart of the West** was one of the earliest entries in the long-running series. John Wayne spent the middle 1930s making B-westerns. Very few posters larger than a one-sheet have survived from any of these films.

Many people consider the one-sheet for **The Oregon Trail** to be the finest John Wayne film poster ever created. In 1991, another copy of this poster was auctioned at Christie's for $10,450.

• 528 **THE OREGON TRAIL,** Republic, 1936, one-sheet, Cond. A, linen backed
41 x 27 in $8,000-10,000

In 1939, Gary Cooper turned down the lead in **Stagecoach** and John Wayne got the role, becoming a superstar after ten years in films. Wayne was not pictured on the one-sheet for **Stagecoach**, but he was featured on the half-sheet offered here.

• 529 **RIDERS OF DESTINY,** Lone Star, 1934, one-sheet, Cond. A, linen backed
41 x 27 in $3,500-4,500

• 530 **THE THREE MUSKETEERS,** Mascot, 1933, one-sheet, Cond. A, linen backed
41 x 27 in $900-1,200

• 531 **STAGECOACH,** United Artists, 1939, half-sheet, Cond. A, unfolded
22 x 28 in $6,000-8,000

Tyrone Power was a major star in 1940, and 20th Century Fox created a stunning one-sheet for **The Mark of Zorro**. Posters from three of James Stewart's greatest film successes are offered here, Many people consider **It's a Wonderful Life** their favorite film.

• 532 **THE MAN WHO SHOT LIBERTY VALANCE,** Paramount, 1962, forty by sixty, Cond. B, unfolded
60 x 40 in $400-600

• 533 **THE MARK OF ZORRO,** 20th Century Fox, 1940, one-sheet, Cond. B, linen backed
41 x 27 in $6,000-8,000

• 534 **THE PHILADELPHIA STORY,** MGM,1940, jumbo window card, Cond. B, folded
28 x 22 in $600-800

• 535 **IT'S A WONDERFUL LIFE,** RKO, 1946, one-sheet, Cond. A, linen backed
41 x 27 in $3,000-4,000

Paramount was not sure how the country would take to The Marx Brothers and their zany humor. They tried to hedge their bet by presenting **The Cocoanuts** as a musical comedy, giving equal billing to sexy dancing girls. The result is perhaps the visually most impressive Marx Brothers poster.

• 536 **THE COCOANUTS,** Paramount, 1929, one-sheet, Cond. A, linen backed
41 x 27 in $9,000-12,000

Duck Soup is one of the best loved of The Marx Brothers' films. The one-sheet offered here has the added distinction of having been personally signed by Groucho.

• 537 **DUCK SOUP,** Paramount, 1933,
one-sheet (autographed by Groucho), Cond. A, paper backed
41 x 27 in $8,000-10,000

• 538 **A NIGHT AT THE OPERA,** MGM, 1935,
jumbo window card, Cond. A
28 x 22 in $4,000-6,000

• 539 **SAILORS, BEWARE!**, Pathe, 1927,
one-sheet, Cond. A, linen backed
41 x 27 in $4,000-6,000

• 540 **THICKER THAN WATER,** MGM, 1935,
three-sheet, Cond. A, linen backed
81 x 41 in $4,000-6,000

Sailors, Beware! has the unusual distinction of being the very first film poster known to feature both Stan Laurel and Oliver Hardy. At the time of the film's production, the two were not a team. Laurel was the star of the movie, while Hardy merely had a supporting role. The unknown poster artist fortunately chose an image that included the two actors who would go on to be the greatest comedy duo of all time.

All the major studios made large forty by sixty silkscreen posters for all their films throughout the 1930s, yet virtually none are known to exist. The one which is offered here is not only from one of Laurel and Hardy's best films, but it is also in excellent condition.

• 541 **OUR RELATIONS,** MGM, 1936,
forty by sixty, Cond. A, unfolded
60 x 40 in

$4,000-6,000

The unusual **Hail Hal Roach!** poster offered here brings together Laurel and Hardy, Our Gang, Charlie Chase, and many others in a single poster, with art by the legendary Al Hirschfeld.

• 542 **A CHUMP AT OXFORD**, United Artists, 1940, one-sheet, Cond. A, linen backed
41 x 27 in $900-1,200

• 543 **SONS OF THE DESERT**, Film Classics, 1947 reissue, one-sheet, Cond. A, linen backed $800-1,000

• 544 **HAIL HAL ROACH!**, MGM, 1934, one-sheet, Cond. B, linen backed
41 x 27 in $900-1,200

• 545 **LUNCHEON AT TWELVE,** MGM, 1933, one-sheet, Cond. A, linen backed
41 x 27 in $700-900

One-sheets from the Our Gang films of the early 1930s are virtually non-existent, with only a handful known.

The posters for **The Wizard of Oz** are highly desired by collectors, especially the title lobby card offered here.

• 546 **BEDTIME WORRIES,** MGM, 1933, one-sheet, Cond. A, linen backed
41 x 27 in $1,800-2,400

• 547 **YE OLDE MINSTRELS,** MGM, 1941, one-sheet, Cond. A, linen backed
41 x 27 in $600-800

• 548 **THE WIZARD OF OZ,** MGM, 1939, title lobby card, Cond. A
11 x 14 in $5,000-7,000

• 549 **HOW TO RAISE A BABY,** MGM, 1938, one-sheet, Cond. A, linen backed
41 x 27 in $800-1,000

• 550 **DARK MAGIC,** MGM, 1939, one-sheet, Cond. B, linen backed
41 x 27 in $700-900

• 551 **ELMER, THE GREAT**, First National, 1932, one-sheet, Cond. A, paper backed
41 x 27 in $1,500-2,000

• 552 **BROAD MINDED**, First National, 1931, one-sheet, Cond. B, linen backed
41 x 27 in $800-1,200

Charlie Chaplin was the greatest star of the silent cinema. He made two memorable films in the 1930s, **City Lights** and **Modern Times**.

• 553 **EASY STREET**, Mutual, 1917, window card, Cond. B, linen backed
20 x 14 in $2,000-3,000

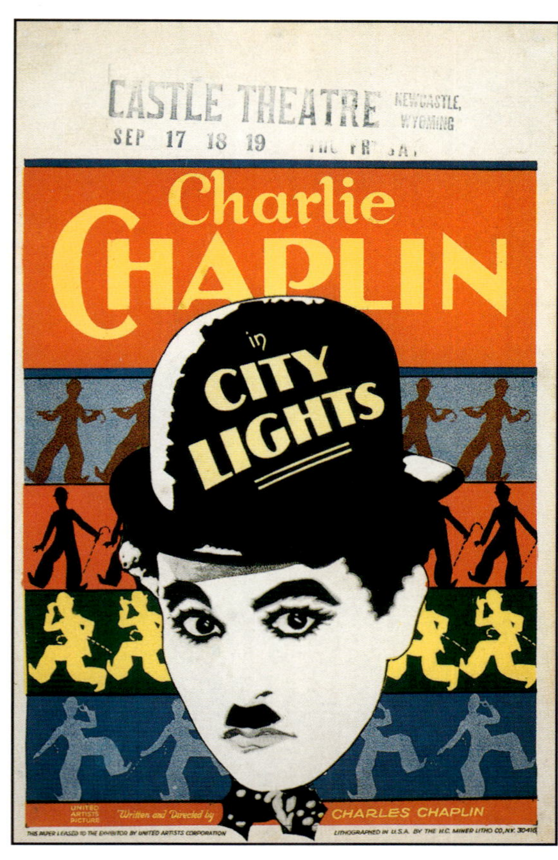

• 554 **CITY LIGHTS**, United Artists, 1931, window card, Cond. A
22 x 14 in $2,500-3,500

The poster for **Modern Times** offered here was created by a midwest company that was in business for only two years, but created several memorable posters.

• 555 **MODERN TIMES**, United Artists, 1936, special poster, Cond. A
60 x 40 in $4,000-6,000

• 556 **DR. JACK**, Pathe, 1922, one-sheet, Cond. A
41 x 27 in $2,500-3,500

Preston Sturges was Hollywood's hottest director in the early 1940s. Apparently, **The Great McGinty** was to have been released as **Down With McGinty**, but the title was changed just before the opening. The studio used the old posters, but changed the title by pasting over the old title!

• 557 **THE GREAT McGINTY** (Down with McGinty), Paramount, 1940, one-sheet, Cond. B, linen backed (with removable snipe)
41 x 27 in $900-1,200

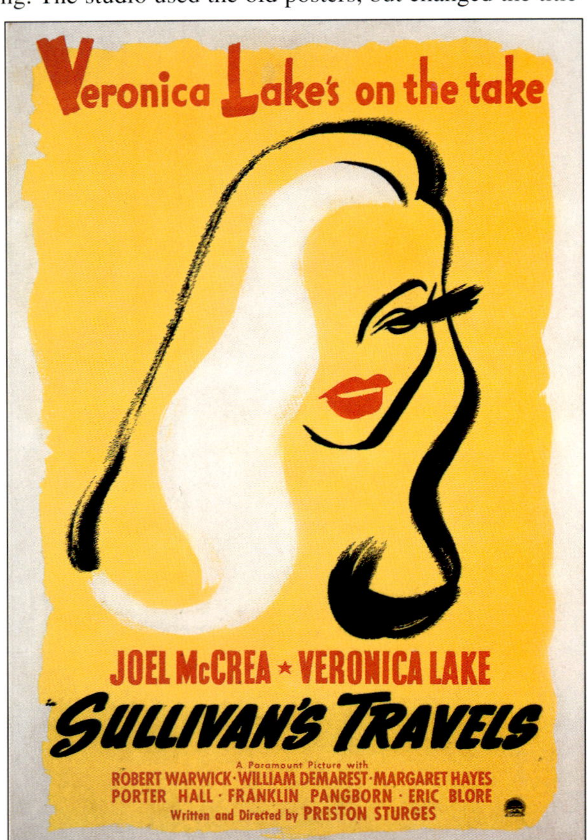

• 558 **SULLIVAN'S TRAVELS**, Paramount, 1941, one-sheet, Cond. A, linen backed
41 x 27 in $1,500-2,000

• 559 **COLLEGE SWING**, Paramount, 1938, three-sheet, Cond. A, linen backed
81 x 41 in $900-1,200

• 560 **GOING SPANISH**, Fox, 1934, one-sheet, Cond. A
41 x 27 in $600-800

W.C. Fields' most memorable screen pairings were those with Mae West (in **My Little Chickadee**) and Charlie McCarthy (in **You Can't Cheat an Honest Man**.) Fields' repartee reached new levels when given an adversary who could trade barbs with him on an equal footing.

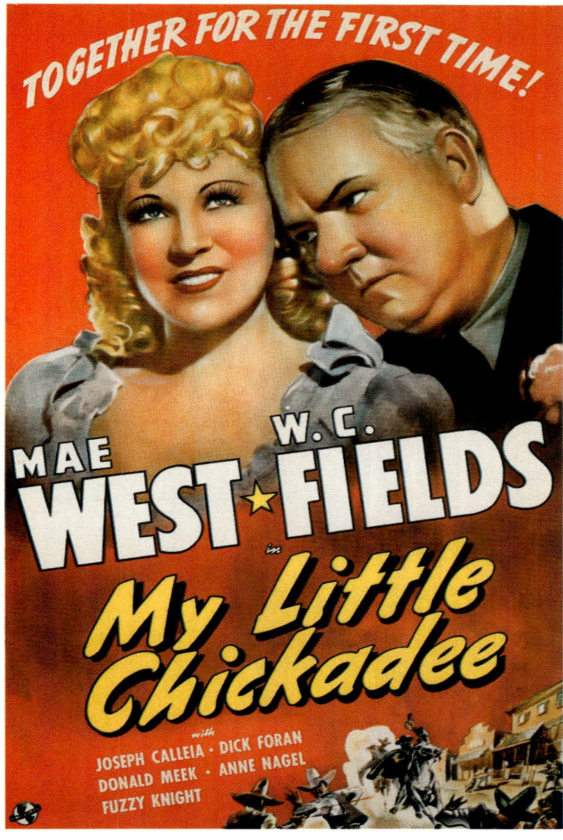

• 561 **MY LITTLE CHICKADEE**, Universal, 1940, one-sheet, Cond. A, linen backed
41 x 27 in $4,000-6,000

• 562 **YOU CAN'T CHEAT AN HONEST MAN**, Universal, 1939, one-sheet, Cond. A, linen backed
41 x 27 in $2,000-3,000

• 563 **CHARLIE McCARTHY, DETECTIVE**, Universal, 1939, one-sheet, Cond. A, linen backed
41 x 27 in $500-700

• 564 **YOU CAN'T CHEAT AN HONEST MAN**, Universal, 1939, one-sheet, Cond. A
41 x 27 in $2,000-3,000

There are many who consider **Singin' in the Rain** the finest movie musical ever made. A magnificent previously unknown standee is offered here. Audrey Hepburn is one of the best loved stars of the 1950s and 1960s, and **Breakfast at Tiffany's** is the most desired of her posters.

• 565 **SINGIN' IN THE RAIN**, MGM, 1952, standee, Cond. A
78 x 46 in $2,000-3,000

• 566 **BREAKFAST AT TIFFANY'S**, Paramount, 1961, one-sheet, Cond. A, linen backed
41 x 27 in $1,000-1,500

• 567 **FUNNY FACE**, Paramount, 1957, standee, Cond. B
58 x 32 in $500-700

• 568 **RIVER OF NO RETURN**, 20th Century Fox, 1954, French poster, Cond. A, linen backed
63 x 47 in $1,200-1,600

Marilyn Monroe is among the greatest stars that the cinema has ever produced. Four of the best posters from her films are offered here, including the memorable skirt-blowing image from **The Seven Year Itch**.

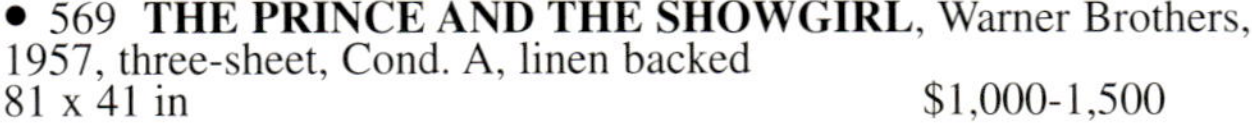

• 569 **THE PRINCE AND THE SHOWGIRL**, Warner Brothers, 1957, three-sheet, Cond. A, linen backed
81 x 41 in $1,000-1,500

• 570 **THE SEVEN YEAR ITCH**, 20th Century Fox, 1955, thirty by forty, Cond. B, paper backed
40 x 30 in $2,000-3,000

• 571 **HOW TO MARRY A MILLIONAIRE**, 20th Century Fox, 1953, British quad, Cond. A
30 x 40 in $700-900

Pro Football was a short subject about the exploits of "Red" Grange and the Chicago Bears. Most short subjects did not have individual posters and the few that did have usually not survived. **The Spirit of Notre Dame** included appearances by The Four Horsemen and was dedicated to Knute Rockne.

• 572 **PRO FOOTBALL**, MGM, 1934, one-sheet, Cond. A
41 x 27 in $900-1,200

• 573 **THE SPIRIT OF NOTRE DAME**, Universal, 1931, one-sheet, Cond. A, linen backed
41 x 27 in $3,000-5,000

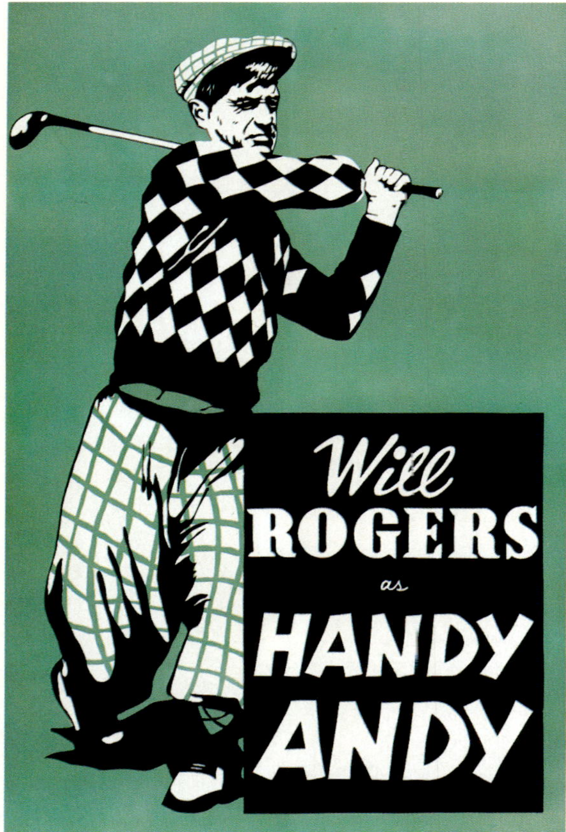

• 574 **HANDY ANDY**, Fox, 1934, Leader Press one-sheet, Cond. A, linen backed
41 x 27 in $700-900

• 575 **TAKING THE COUNT**, Vitaphone, 1937, one-sheet, Cond. A, linen backed
41 x 27 in $800-1,000

Douglas Fairbanks was the silent cinema's greatest action star and **Robin Hood** was one of his most memorable roles. It is not surprising this film received a gorgeous poster, as Fairbanks was a co-owner of United Artists, which made the film!

• 576 **ROBIN HOOD**, United Artists, 1921, one-sheet, Cond. A, linen backed
41 x 27 in $15,000-20,000

The Black Pirate was another memorable Fairbanks film which received a knockout poster. It must be seen in person to be appreciated. Modern printing techniques cannot fully capture the colors and texture of stone lithography.

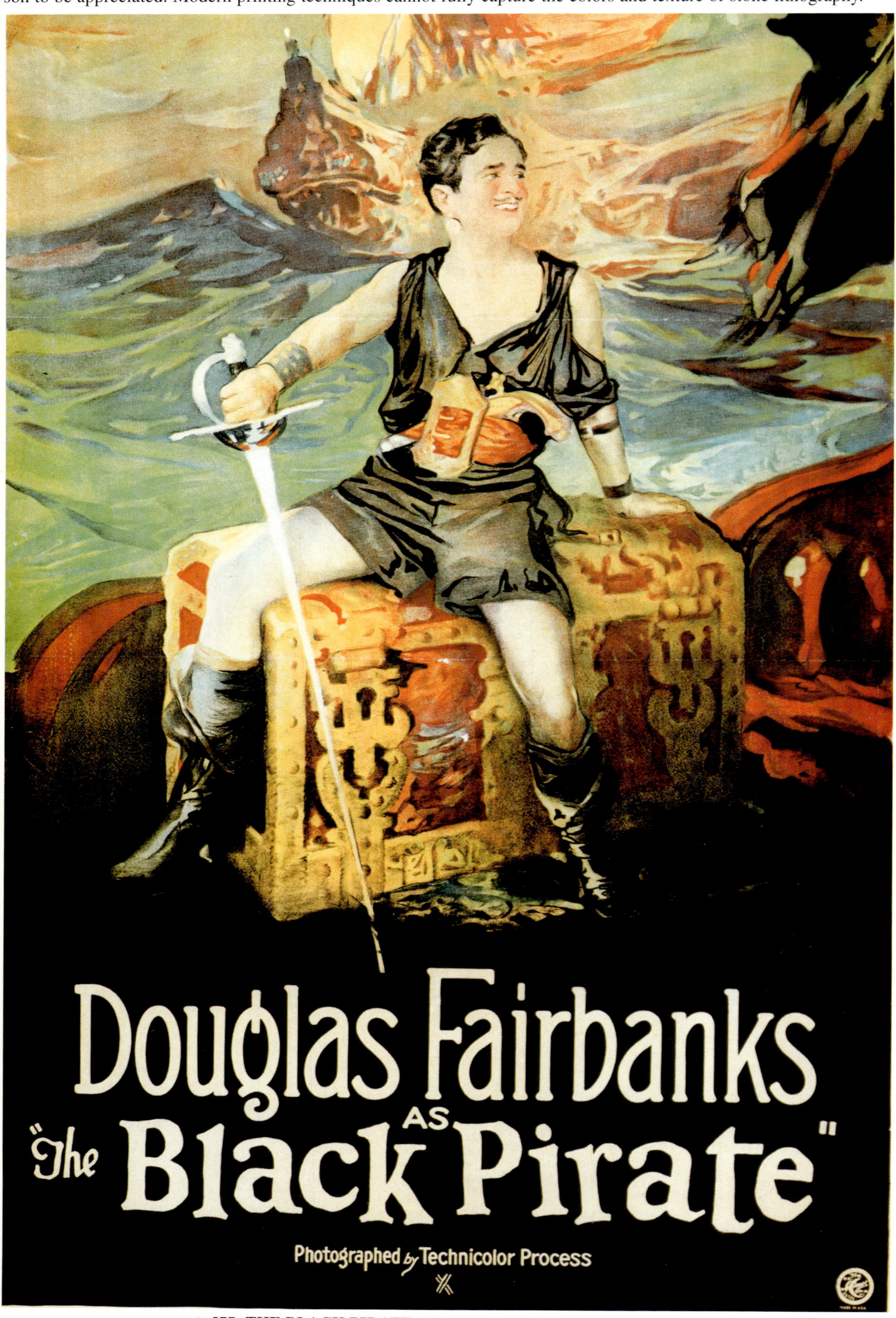

• 577 **THE BLACK PIRATE,** United Artists, 1926, one-sheet, Cond. A, linen backed
41 x 27 in

$10,000-15,000

Many people consider Rudolph Valentino's last film, **The Son of the Shiek**, to also be his finest. United Artists delivered a magnificent one-sheet, which captures Valentino's raw sex appeal.

• 578 **THE SON OF THE SHEIK**, Paramount, 1926, one-sheet, Cond. B, paper backed
41 x 27 in $10,000-15,000

Errol Flynn became an instant superstar with his first American film, **Captain Blood**. Audiences loved to see him in action roles, but unfortunately the excesses of his private life cut short his career.

• 579 **A SAINTED DEVIL**, Paramount, 1924, window card, Cond. A, linen backed
22 x 14 in $1,000-1,500

• 580 **BEAU GESTE,** Paramount, 1939, one-sheet, Cond. A
41 x 27 in $4,000-6,000

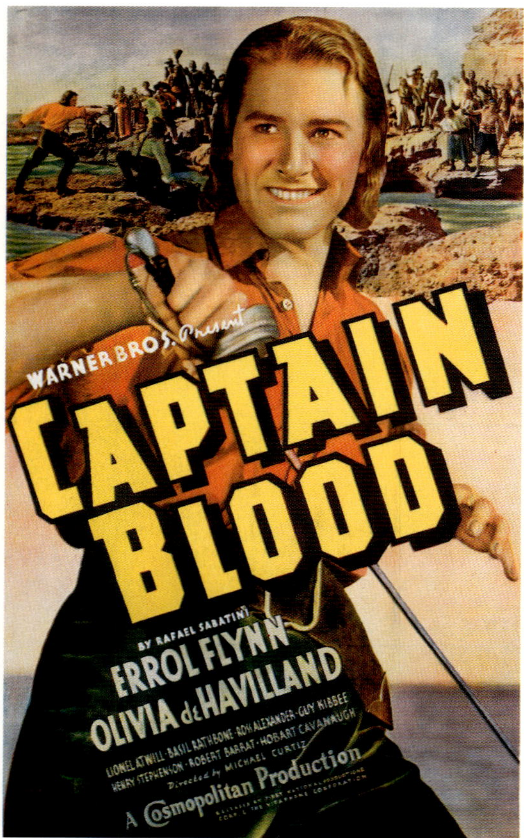

• 581 **CAPTAIN BLOOD**, Warner Brothers, 1935, one-sheet, Cond. A, linen backed
41 x 27 in $6,000-8,000

• 582 **THE SEA HAWK**, Warner Brothers, 1940, one-sheet, Cond. B, linen backed
41 x 27 in $3,000-4,000

The Adventures of Robin Hood was Errol Flynn's masterpiece, and one of the best-loved films of the 1930s. Each poster from this film had a totally different image, and two of the best of these are offered here.

• 583 **THE ADVENTURES OF ROBIN HOOD**, Warner Brothers, 1938, half-sheet, Cond. B, linen backed
22 x 28 in $6,000-8,000

• 584 **THE ADVENTURES OF ROBIN HOOD**, Warner Brothers, 1938, window card, Cond. B, paper backed
22 x 14 in $1,500-2,000

• 585 **THE DAWN PATROL**, Warner Brothers, 1938, jumbo window card, Cond. A
28 x 22 in $2,000-3,000

The most famous movie monsters were drawn from classic literature. The main exception is **King Kong**, perhaps the most famous, and certainly the biggest monster of them all. Although there have been massive strides in the field of special effects in recent years, the overall effect of Willis O'Brien's stop-action photography has not been equalled.

The three-sheet poster offered here combines the most important elements one looks for in a movie poster. It is from a classic film, it is magnificently rendered, and it depicts the most memorable scene from the film, one of the best remembered images in the history of film.

No restoration has been performed on this poster, both so that prospective buyers can see what excellent condition the poster is in, and so that the purchaser may choose how best to preserve this piece of film history.

• 586 **KING KONG**, RKO, 1933, three-sheet, Cond. A
81 x 41 in $70,000-90,000

Posters from the major Universal horror films of the early 1930s are very scarce, and few ever come up for sale or auction. The one-sheet poster for **The Invisible Man** offered here is the advance or "teaser" style, designed to be displayed prior to a film's release.

• 587 **THE INVISIBLE MAN**, Universal, 1933, advance one-sheet, Cond. B, linen backed
41 x 27 in $40,000-60,000

Dracula was Universal Pictures' first major sound horror film, and lobby cards from **Dracula** are the most desired of Universal's films. An entire set of eight lobby cards is offered here. Not only are the cards very rare, but each depicts a totally different, yet striking and desirable scene from the film.

• 588 **DRACULA**, Universal, 1931,
lobby card, Cond. A
11 x 14 in $800-1,200

• 589 **DRACULA**, Universal, 1931,
lobby card, Cond. A
11 x 14 in $3,000-4,000

• 590 **DRACULA**, Universal, 1931,
lobby card, Cond. A
11 x 14 in $5,000-7,000

• 591 **DRACULA**, Universal, 1931,
lobby card, Cond. A
11 x 14 in $5,000-7,000

• 592 **DRACULA**, Universal, 1931,
lobby card, Cond. A
11 x 14 in $6,000-8,000

• 593 **DRACULA**, Universal, 1931,
lobby card, Cond. A
11 x 14 in $7,000-9,000

• 594 **DRACULA**, Universal, 1931, lobby card, Cond. A
11 x 14 in $7,000-9,000

• 595 **DRACULA**, Universal, 1931, title lobby card, Cond. A
11 x 14 in $10,000-15,000

• 596 **THE GHOST OF FRANKENSTEIN**, Universal, 1942, one-sheet, Cond. A, linen backed
41 x 27 in $5,000-7,000

• 597 **FRANKENSTEIN MEETS THE WOLF MAN**, Universal, 1943, one-sheet, Cond. B, linen backed
41 x 27 in $2,000-3,000

• 598 **FRANKENSTEIN MEETS THE WOLF MAN**, Universal, 1943, three-sheet, Cond. A, linen backed
81 x 41 in $5,000-7,000

The success of **Frankenstein** spawned a large number of sequels. The two of these from the 1940s that have the best images and are the most desired are **The Ghost of Frankenstein** and **Frankenstein Meets the Wolf Man.**

• 599 **THE DAY THE EARTH STOOD STILL**, 20th Century Fox, 1951, six-sheet, Cond. A, linen backed
81 x 81 in $9,000-12,000

The first and best of the great 1950s science fiction films was **The Day the Earth Stood Still**. While the smaller size posters are readily obtainable, the six-sheet poster is very rare and has never before been offered at auction.

• 600 **DER HERR DER WELT**, Tobis, 1934, German poster, Cond. A, linen backed
56 x 37in $5,000-7,000

• 601 **TARANTULA**, Universal, 1955, forty by sixty, Cond. A, unfolded
60 x 40 in $900-1,200

• 602 **MYSTERIOUS MR. WONG**, Monogram, 1935, one-sheet, Cond. A
41 x 27 in $900-1,200

• 603 **FORBIDDEN PLANET**, MGM, 1956, insert, Cond. A, unfolded
36 x 14 in $1,000-1,500

Der Herr Der Welt was a German film that has a poster with a spectacular image of a robot. **Forbidden Planet** is probably most famous for introducing Robbie the Robot.

In the 1920s and 1930s, African-Americans were often forced to work in all-black films because mainstream films were closed to them. One exception was Paul Robeson, who also made films in England, including **The Proud Valley**, for which the only known British quad is offered here.

• 604 **HARLEM IS HEAVEN,** 1932,
one-sheet, Cond. B, linen backed
41 x 27 in $700-900

• 605 **GONE HARLEM**, Creative Cinema, 1939,
one-sheet, Cond. A
41 x 27 in $700-900

• 606 **SHOW BOAT,** Universal, 1936,
twelve lobby cards (four pictured), Cond. A, (two cards Cond. B)
each 11 x 14 in $1,200-1,600

• 607 **THE PROUD VALLEY**, A.B.F.D., 1939,
British quad, Cond. A, linen backed
30 x 40 in $900-1,200

Many people do not realize that there were sound Sherlock Holmes films prior to those of Basil Rathbone. **Blackmail** was Alfred Hitchcock's very first talking film.

• 608 **THE RETURN OF SHERLOCK HOLMES**, Paramount, 1929, insert, Cond. B, linen backed
36 x 14 in $900-1,200

• 609 **THE SIGN OF FOUR**, Cinema Art, 1932, Australian daybill, Cond. B
40 x 15 in $600-800

• 610 **BLACKMAIL**, Cinema Art, 1929, Australian daybill, Cond. B
40 x 15 in $2,000-3,000

• 611 **THE CANARY MURDER CASE**, Paramount, 1929, Swedish poster, Cond. A, unfolded
35 x 23 in $1,200-1,600

• 612 **CHARLIE CHAN'S CHANCE**, Fox, 1932, one-sheet, Cond. A, linen backed
41 x 27 in $1,500-2,000

The quality of poster art generally diminished in the 1940s, but happily there were significant exceptions. Perhaps the finest poster images of the 1940s are offered on this page.

• 613 **THIS GUN FOR HIRE**, Paramount, 1942, one-sheet, Cond. A, linen backed
41 x 27 in $5,000-7,000

• 614 **OUT OF THE PAST**, RKO, 1947, one-sheet, Cond. B, linen backed
41 x 27 in $2,000-3,000

• 615 **GILDA**, Columbia, 1946, one-sheet, Cond. B, paper backed
41 x 27 in $4,000-6,000

• 616 **THE LADY FROM SHANGHAI**, Columbia, 1948, insert, Cond. A, linen backed
36 x 14 in $1,000-1,500

Poll after poll has acclaimed **Citizen Kane** as the finest film ever made. While most of the posters from the film are obtainable, the rare "B-style" one-sheet virtually never comes up for sale. An excellent copy is offered here.

• 617 **CITIZEN KANE**, RKO, 1941, one-sheet, Cond. A, paper backed
41 x 27 in

$17,000-22,000

• 618 **CASABLANCA**, Warner Brothers, 1942,
insert, Cond. B, linen backed
36 x 14 in $6,000-8,000

Humphrey Bogart was the star of some of the most critically acclaimed and best-loved films ever made, and not surprisingly, posters from these films are highly prized.

• 619 **THE MALTESE FALCON**, Warner Brothers, 1941,
one-sheet, Cond. B, linen backed
41 x 27 in $4,000-6,000

• 620 **THE AFRICAN QUEEN**, United Artists, 1951,
six-sheet, Cond. A, linen backed
81 x 81 in $3,000-4,000

While the quality of films and posters generally declined in the 1940s, there were still many examples of films or posters that are on a par with those of the 1930s, and these are avidly sought by collectors.

• 621 **SHERLOCK HOLMES AND THE VOICE OF TERROR**, Universal, 1942, one-sheet, Cond. B, linen backed
41 x 27 in $800-1,000

• 622 **I LOVE TROUBLE**, Columbia, 1947, one-sheet, Cond. A, linen backed
41 x 27 in $400-600

• 623 **THE THIRD MAN**, Selznick, 1949, one-sheet, Cond. A
41 x 27 in $600-800

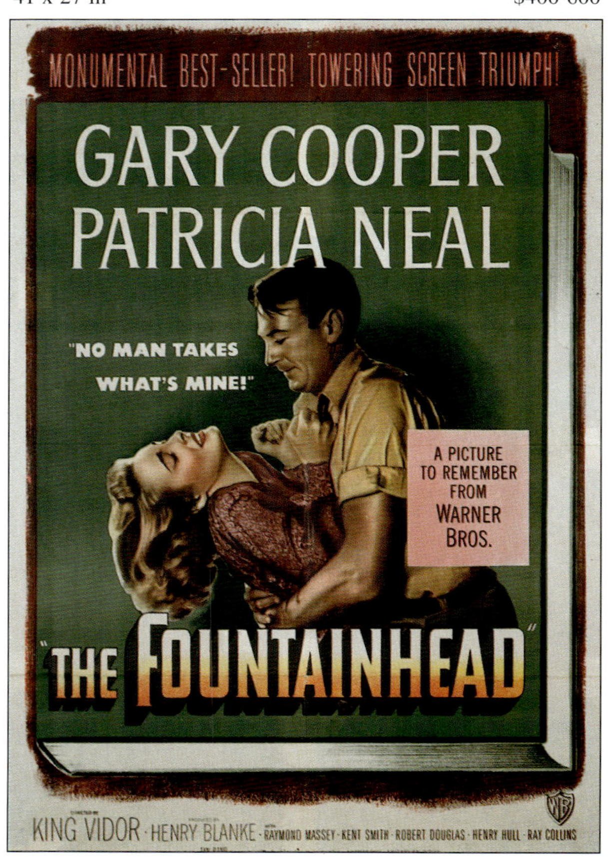

• 624 **THE FOUNTAINHEAD**, Warner Brothers, 1949, one-sheet, Cond. A
41 x 27 in $600-800

One of the most important musicals of the early 1930s was **Flying Down to Rio**. It not only elevated the movie musical to an art form, but it also introduced the dance team of Fred Astaire and Ginger Rogers. An exceptional copy of the one-sheet is offered here.

• 625 **FLYING DOWN TO RIO**, RKO, 1933,
one-sheet, Cond. A, linen backed
41 x 27 in $9,000-12,000

Shirley Temple is certainly the greatest child star of all time. **Baby, Take a Bow** was one of her earliest starring roles, and **Dimples** was one of her most successful films.

• 626 **BABY, TAKE A BOW**, Fox, 1934,
one-sheet, Cond. A, linen backed
41 x 27 in $3,000-4,000

• 627 **DIMPLES**, 20th Century Fox, 1936,
one-sheet, Cond. A, linen backed
41 x 27 in $2,000-3,000

• 628 **FIFTY DOLLAR BILL**, Vitaphone, 1935,
one-sheet, Cond. B
41 x 27 in $400-600

• 629 **FOOTLIGHT PARADE**, Warner Brothers, 1933,
window card, Cond. A
22 x 14 in $6,000-8,000

Gold Diggers of 1933 and **Footlight Parade** were made at Warner Brothers at the same time **Flying Down to Rio** was made at RKO. The Warner Brothers films showcased the artistry of Busby Berkeley, whose films were never surpassed.

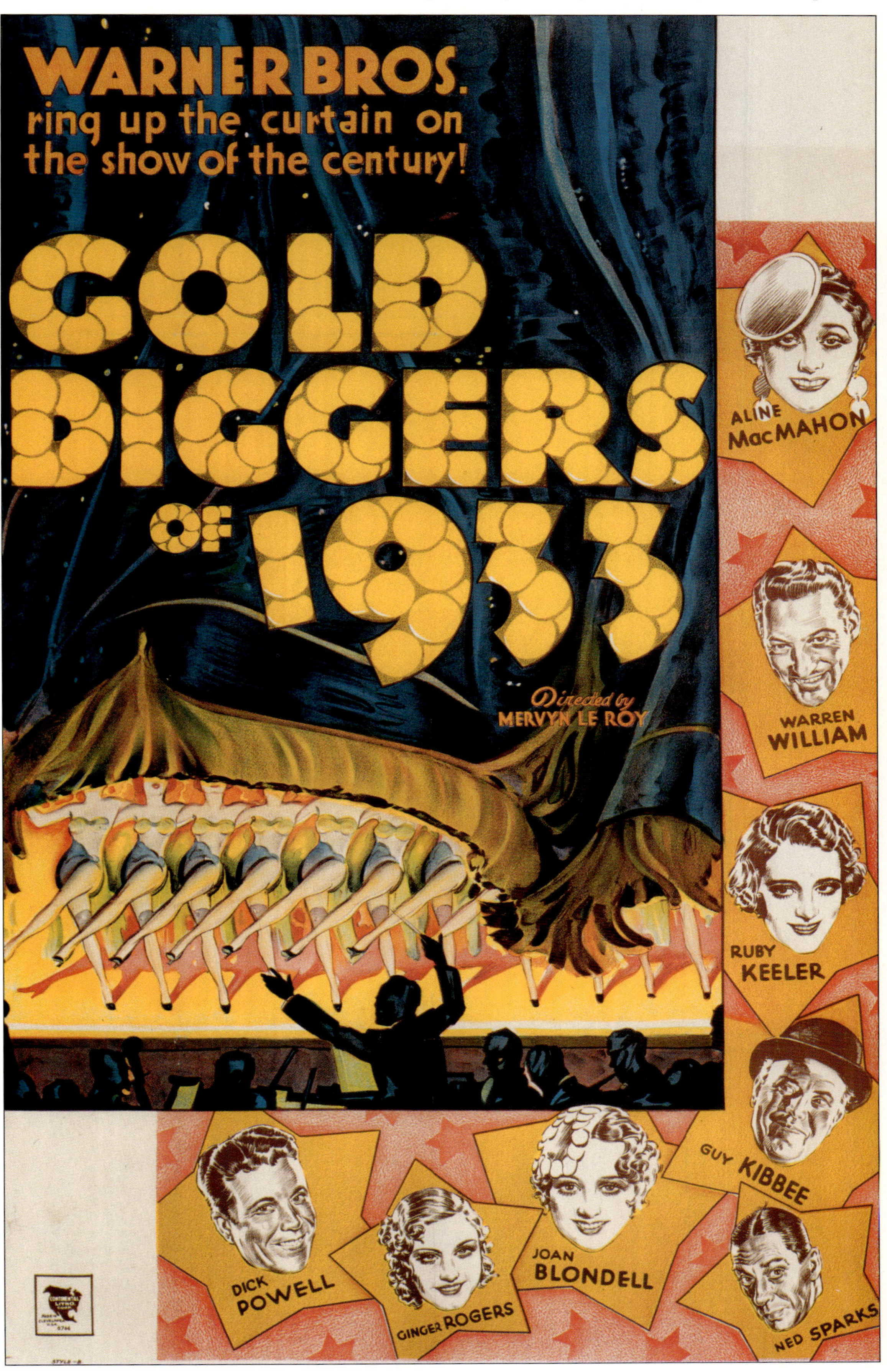

• 630 **GOLD DIGGERS OF 1933**, Warner Brothers, 1933, one-sheet, Cond. A, paper backed
41 x 27 in $9,000-12,000

Every major studio made a special silkscreen size poster called a thirty by forty, for every film from the 1930s on. Similar in size to one-sheets, they were printed on much thicker paper and cost ten times as much. Perhaps this is why not a single thirty by forty has ever surfaced from the 1930s until now. How fortunate that the one offered here, **Follow the Fleet**, is not only from a major film, but is also in excellent condition.

• 631 **FOLLOW THE FLEET**, RKO, 1936,
thirty by forty, Cond. A
40 x 30 in

$5,000-7,000

• 632 **THE GAY DIVORCEE**, RKO, 1934,
one-sheet (autographed by Astaire), Cond. A, paper backed
41 x 27 in $6,000-8,000

• 633 **TANNED LEGS**, Radio (RKO), 1929,
one-sheet, Cond. B, linen backed
41 x 27 $1,500-2,000

Jeanette MacDonald is best-remembered today for her dignified pairings in operettas with Nelson Eddy, but earlier she was a sexy leading lady in films such as **The Vagabond King** and **The Love Parade**.

• 634 **THE LOVE PARADE**, Paramount, 1929,
insert, Cond. B, linen backed
36 x 14 in $500-700

• 635 **THE VAGABOND KING**, Paramount, 1930,
one-sheet, Cond. A, linen backed
41 x 27 in $1,000-1,500

The Birth of a Nation is one of the most critically acclaimed, yet controversial films of all time. Based on the novel, **The Clansman**, it had been believed that the title was changed prior to the film's release to avoid controversy. Yet offered here is both a window card from the regular release, as well as one for a release as **The Clansman**, proving it was released under both titles.

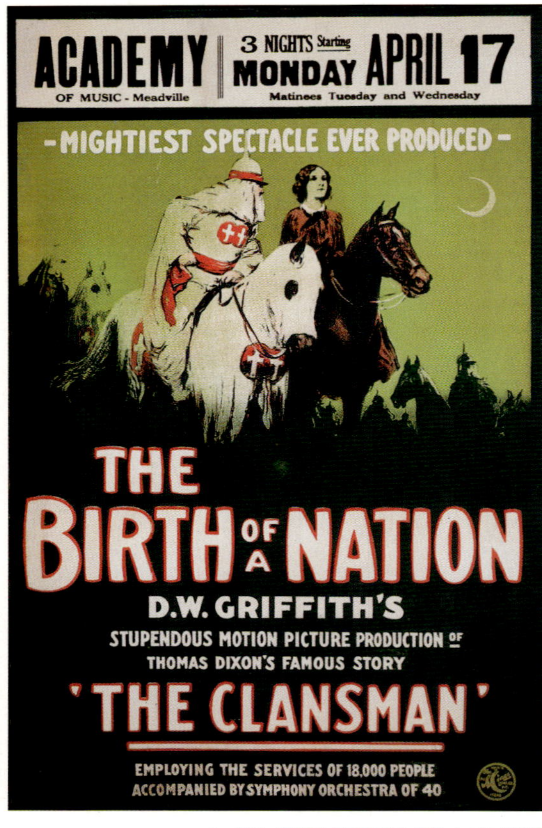

• 636 **THE BIRTH OF A NATION** and **THE CLANSMAN**, D.W. Griffith, 1915,
two window cards, Cond. A and Cond. B, paper backed
each 22 x 14 in $17,000-22,000

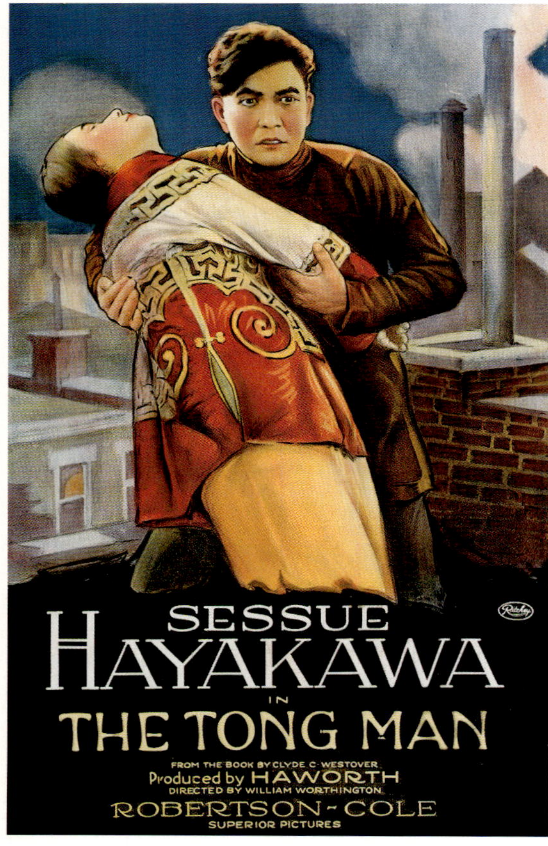

• 637 **THE TONG MAN**, Haworth, 1919,
one-sheet, Cond. A, linen backed
41 x 27 in $2,000-3,000

• 638 **THE EAGLE'S EYE**, Whartons, 1918,
one-sheet, Cond. A, linen backed
41 x 27 in $500-700

• 639 **ENOCH ARDEN,** Biograph, 1911, three-sheet, Cond. B, linen backed
81 x 41 in $3,000-4,000

Universal Studios opened its studio in California in 1915. It maintained a zoo and well-stocked backlot, not only for its own films, but for those of other studios, which paid a rental fee. Many decades later, Universal City is a major Hollywood attraction.

• 640 **UNIVERSAL CITY CALIFORNIA**, Universal, 1915, one-sheet, Cond. A, linen backed
41 x 27 in $4,000-6,000

• 641 **LONDON**, Paramount, 1927, one-sheet, Cond. A, linen backed
41 x 27 in $1,000-1,500

The posters for films of the 1920s were almost always artistically appealing. The posters for Hollywood's biggest stars were created by the studios' finest artists. The poster for **Salome** was created by Aubrey Beardsley.

• 642 **HER HUSBAND'S TRADEMARK**, Paramount, 1922, one-sheet, Cond. B, linen backed
41 x 27 in $4,500-6,500

• 643 **THE SIN SISTER**, William Fox, 1929, one-sheet, Cond. A, linen backed
41 x 27 in $600-800

• 644 **SALOME**, Allied Producers, 1922, one-sheet, Cond. A, linen backed
41 x 27 in $4,000-6,000

• 645 **BLUE SKIES**, William Fox, 1929, one-sheet, Cond. A, linen backed
41 x 27 in $500-700

In 1919, Robert Wiene directed a film in Germany, **The Cabinet of Dr. Caligari**, that revolutionized the cinema with its innovative techniques. In 1921, Samuel Goldwyn exhibited the film in the United States. Another copy of this one-sheet was auctioned at Christie's in 1990 for $37,400, setting the world record price for a movie poster at that time.

• 646 **THE CABINET OF DR. CALIGARI**, Goldwyn, 1921, one-sheet, Cond. A, linen backed
41 x 27 in $35,000-50,000

The beautifully rendered one-sheet for **A Romance of the Redwoods** is from a film that not only starred Mary Pickford, but was directed by the legendary Cecil B. DeMille.

• 647 **A ROMANCE OF THE REDWOODS**, Artcraft, 1917, one-sheet, Cond. A, linen backed
41 x 27 in $3,000-4,000

• 648 **THE FIRST AUTO**, Warner Brothers, 1927, one-sheet, Cond. A, linen backed
41 x 27 in $600-800

• 649 **THE SON OF TARZAN,** National Film, 1920, one-sheet, Cond. A, linen backed
41 x 27 in $800-1,000

• 650 **CHASING THROUGH EUROPE**, William Fox, 1929, one-sheet, Cond. A, linen backed
41 x 27 in $600-800

The one-sheet for **Dante's Inferno** offered here is not from the William Fox silent version or from the Spencer Tracy talking version, but rather from an Italian version imported into the United States in the early 1920s.

• 651 **DANTE'S INFERNO**, Jawitz, circa 1921, one-sheet, Cond. A, linen backed
41 x 27 in $1,500-2,000

• 652 **THE CROWD**, MGM, 1928, window card, Cond. A
22 x 14 in $600-800

• 653 **SOUTH SEA ROSE**, William Fox, 1929, one-sheet, Cond. A, linen backed
41 x 27 in $600-800

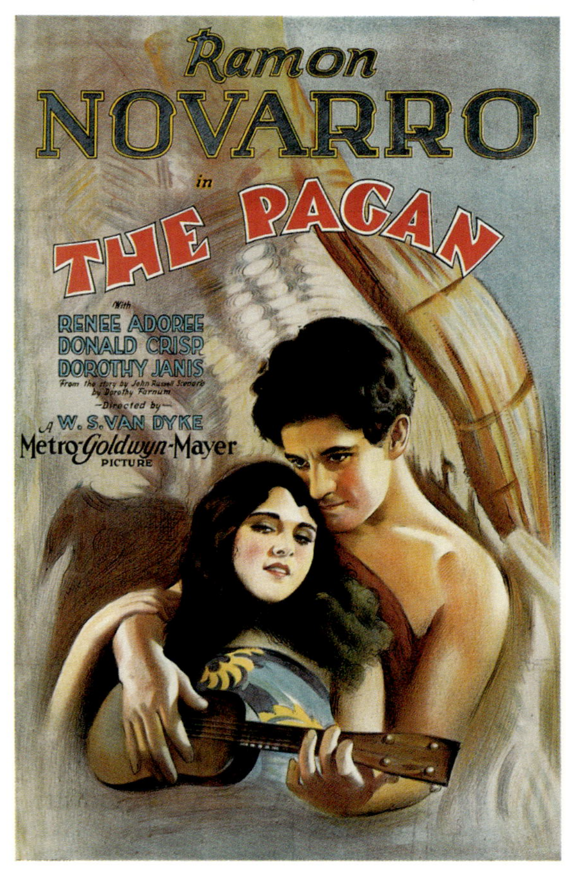

• 654 **THE PAGAN**, MGM, 1929, one-sheet, Cond. A, linen backed
41 x 27 in $800-1,000

• 655 **ADVENTURES OF TARZAN**, Numa Pictures, 1921, six-sheet, Cond. A, linen backed
81 x 81 in $9,000-12,000

Few six-sheets have survived from silent films, and fewer from serial films. Offered here is a six-sheet from **Adventures of Tarzan**, which starred Elmo Lincoln, who had been the very first screen Tarzan.

Posters from the first three MGM Tarzan films (all starring Johnny Weissmuller) are extremely rare. Offered here is the rarer "B-style" one-sheet from the second MGM Tarzan, **Tarzan and His Mate**.

• 656 **TARZAN AND HIS MATE**, MGM, 1934, one-sheet, Cond. A, linen backed
41 x 27 in $6,000-8,000

• 657 **GONE WITH THE WIND**, MGM, 1939,
six-sheet, Cond. A, linen backed
81 x 81 in $30,000-40,000

The most beloved film of all time is **Gone With The Wind**. Because of its enormous popularity, it received three full scale releases in 1939 and 1940 alone, which has resulted in posters from its initial release being extremely rare and highly sought after by collectors. Offered here is the only known copy of the six-sheet from the initial release.

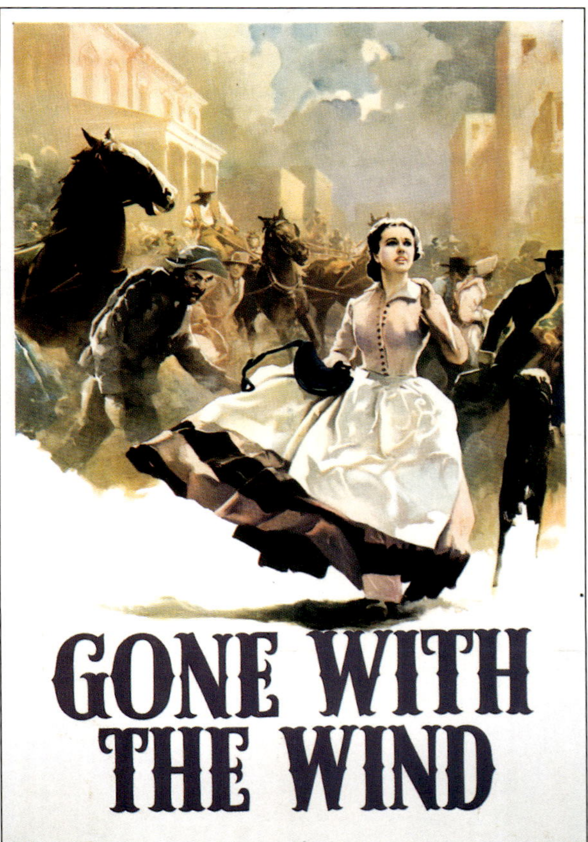

• 658 **GONE WITH THE WIND**, MGM, 1939,
one-sheet, Cond. A, paper backed
41 x 27 in $7,000-9,000

• 659 **GONE WITH THE WIND**, MGM, 1940,
one-sheet, Cond. B, linen backed
41 x 27 in $4,000-6,000

• 660 **GONE WITH THE WIND**, MGM, 1940,
three-sheet, Cond. B, linen backed
81 x 41 in $6,000-8,000

The three posters on this page are from the first three releases of **Gone With The Wind**. Lot 658 is a one-sheet from the 1939 release. Lot 659 is a one-sheet from the first 1940 release ("Nothing Cut! Full Length!"). Lot 660 is a three-sheet from the second 1940 release ("Nothing Cut But The Price!").

In the late 1920s and early 1930s, a genre of films called "bad girl" films became quite popular. It is interesting to note that **Loose Ankles** starred sixteen year-old Loretta Young, in her first starring role.

• 661 **MAN AGAINST WOMAN,** Columbia, 1932, one-sheet, Cond. B
41 x 27 in $700-900

• 662 **LOVER COME BACK**, Columbia, 1931, one-sheet, Cond. A, linen backed
41 x 27 in $700 $900

• 663 **CHILD OF MANHATTAN**, Columbia, 1933, one-sheet, Cond. A, linen backed
41 x 27 in $800-1,000

• 664 **LOOSE ANKLES**, First National, 1929, one-sheet, Cond. A, linen backed
41 x 27 in $700-900

• 665 **EAST IS WEST**, Universal, 1930, one-sheet, Cond. A
41 x 27 in $600-800

• 666 **THE NIGHT RIDE**, Universal, 1930, one-sheet, Cond. A, linen backed
41 x 27 in $800-1,000

Most film buffs think of **Little Caesar** as the great actor Edward G. Robinson's first film role, but he had appeared in a few earlier films, including **East is West** and **The Night Ride**.

• 667 **THE NIGHT RIDE**, Universal, 1930, insert, Cond. A, folded once
36 x 14 in $400-600

• 668 **THE LOST ZEPPELIN**, Tiffany-Stahl, 1929, one-sheet, Cond. A, linen backed
41 x 27 in $900-1,200

Posters from the three Flash Gordon serials are very rare and highly prized by collectors. Offered here is the one-sheet for the entire second serial. This particular copy was autographed by Buster Crabbe, making it even more desirable.

• 669 **FLASH GORDON'S TRIP TO MARS**, Universal, 1938, one-sheet (autographed by Buster Crabbe), Cond. A, linen backed
41 x 27 in $8,000-10,000

One of the most popular areas of movie poster collecting is that of films based on comic strip or comic book heroes. They are most desirable when they feature only art from the source material, as with the **Superman** and **Blondie** posters offered here.

• 670 **FLASH GORDON CONQUERS THE UNIVERSE**, Universal, 1940, one-sheet, Cond. A
41 x 27 in $1,000-1,500

• 671 **SUPERMAN**, Columbia, 1948, advance one-sheet, Cond. B, linen backed
41 x 27 in $2,000-3,000

• 672 **LITTLE ORPHAN ANNIE**, RKO, 1932, seven lobby cards (two pictured), Cond. A
each 11 x 14 in $300-500

• 673 **BLONDIE**, Columbia, 1938, one-sheet, Cond. A
41 x 27 in $1,500-2,000

• 674 **ATOM MAN VS. SUPERMAN**, Columbia, 1950,
six-sheet, Cond. A, linen backed
81 x 81 in $5,000-7,000

It took ten years after his creation for Hollywood to make a live-action Superman film. Called **Superman** (see lot 671), it starred Kirk Alyn, and it spawned a sequel two years later, **Atom Man vs. Superman**. A magnificent six-sheet from that film is offered here.

Disney's first full-length feature film, **Snow White and the Seven Dwarfs**, was released in 1937. Surprisingly, the "A-style" one-sheet pictured only the dwarfs. The much more desirable "B-style" one-sheet, depicting all the major characters, is offered here.

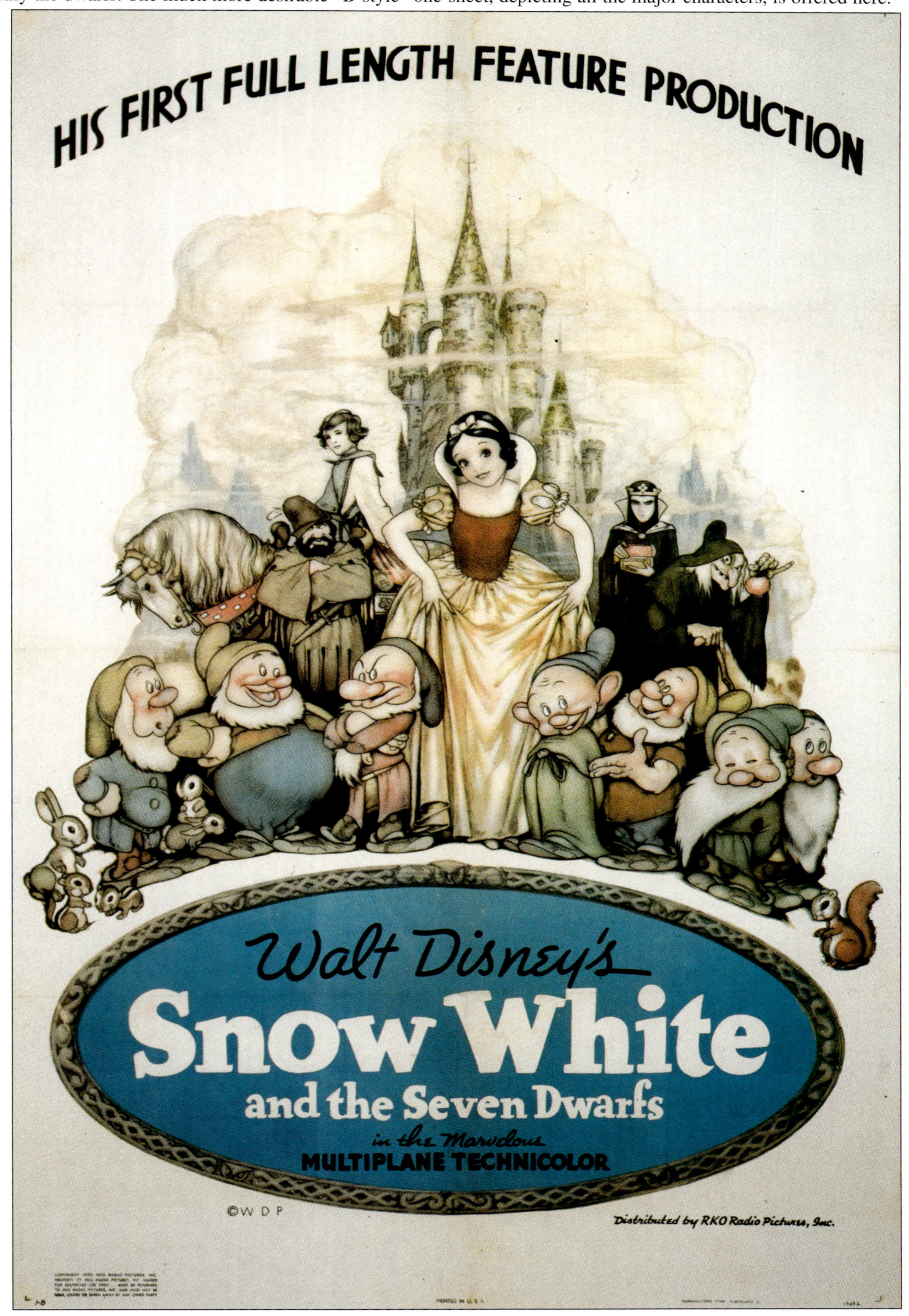

• 675 **SNOW WHITE AND THE SEVEN DWARFS**, RKO, 1937, one-sheet, Cond. A, linen backed
41 x 27 in $10,000-15,000

It didn't take long for the world to fall in love with Mickey Mouse, and his cartoons were soon playing in movie theatres around the world. Four of the earliest French Disney posters, each with a charming image, are offered here.

• 676 **MICKEY GALANT**, Pathe, circa 1930,
French poster, Cond. A, linen backed
47 x 32 in $4,500-6,500

• 677 **MICKEY MELOMANE**, Pathe, circa 1930,
French poster, Cond. A, linen backed
47 x 32 in $4,000-6,000

• 678 **MICKEY MECANO**, Pathe, circa 1930,
French poster, Cond. A, linen backed
47 x 32 in $4,000-6,000

• 679 **MICKEY MARIN**, Pathe, circa 1930,
French poster, Cond. A, linen backed
47 x 32 in $4,000-6,000

• 680 **FANTASIA**, RKO, 1940,
one-sheet, Cond. A, linen backed
41 x 27 in $3,500-5,000

Mickey Mouse starred in a segment of Walt Disney's **Fantasia** in 1940, the first Disney character to cross-over from short to a feature film. Yet, Mickey was soon upstaged by Donald Duck, who became Disney's most popular cartoon star of the 1940s.

682 **NO LOT**

• 681 **FANTASIA**, RKO, 1940,
jumbo window card, Cond. A
28 x 22 in $1,000-1,500

• 683 **A GOOD TIME FOR A DIME**, RKO, 1941,
one-sheet, Cond. A, linen backed
41 x 27 in $2,000-3,000

Warner Brothers had great cartoon stars in the 1930s, but unfortunately chose to make only generic or "stock" posters. However, a marvelous standee, featuring Porky Pig, is offered here.

• 684 **LOONEY TUNES**, Vitaphone, circa 1936, standee, Cond. B, paper backed
48 x 28 in $6,000-8,000

• 685 **A NEW LOONEY TUNES**, Vitaphone, 1941, one-sheet, Cond. A
41 x 27 in $1,500-2,000

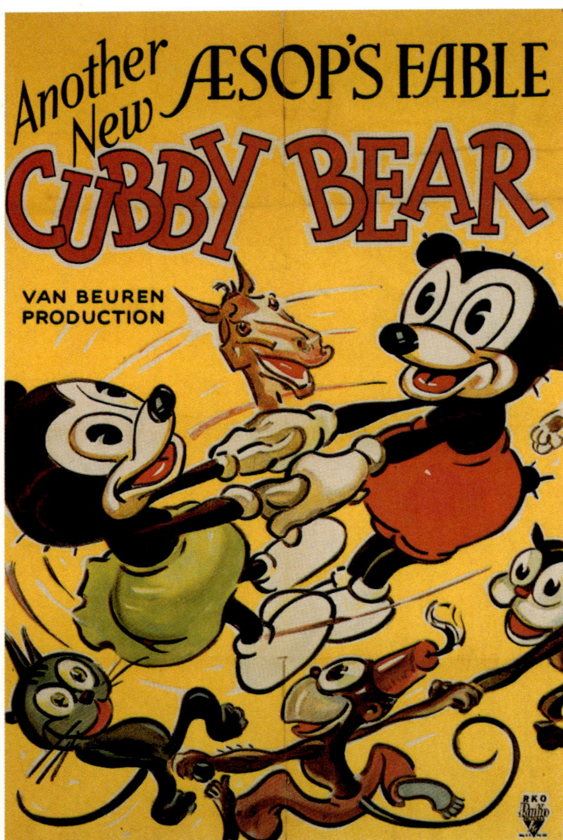

• 686 **CUBBY BEAR**, RKO, circa 1933, one-sheet, Cond. B
41 x 27 in $500-700

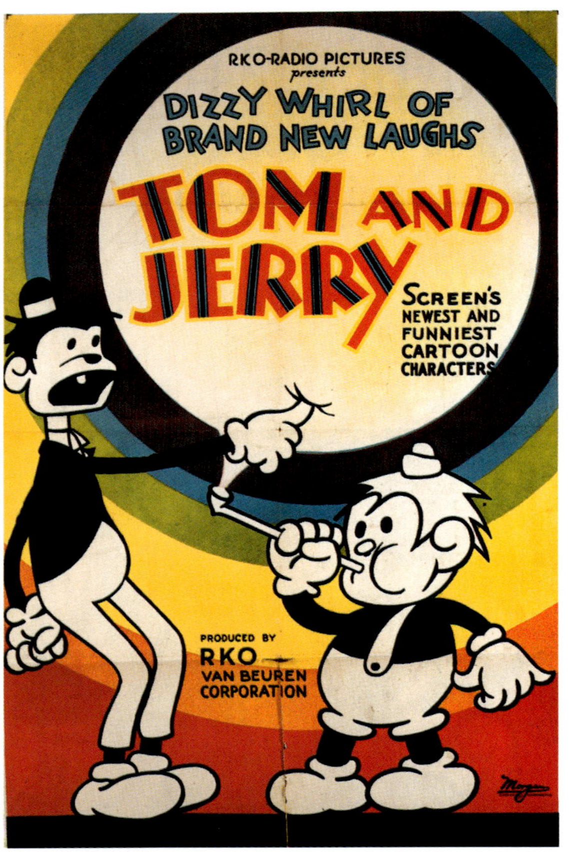

• 687 **TOM AND JERRY**, RKO, circa 1933, one-sheet, Cond. B
41 x 27 in $500-700

Paramount was the studio that had the services of the Fleischer brothers. Probably their greatest creation was Betty Boop. The earliest known poster image of Betty Boop is offered here. It is from before her own series, when she was in Talkartoons, along with Bimbo and Koko the Clown.

• 688 **CUPID GETS SOME NEW DOPE**, Powers, 1917, one-sheet, Cond. B, framed
41 x 27 in $1,000-1,500

• 689 **ANOTHER NEW PARAMOUNT TALKARTOON**, Paramount, circa 1932, one-sheet, Cond. A
41 x 27 in $3,500-5,000

• 690 **ANOTHER NEW PARAMOUNT SCREEN SONG**, Paramount, circa 1932, one-sheet, Cond. A
41 x 27 in $900-1,200

• 691 **MR. BUG GOES TO TOWN**, Paramount, 1941, half-sheet, Cond. B, paper backed, unfolded
22 x 28 in $600-800

Clark Gable had a real-life torrid romance with Carole Lombard, but unfortunately, they only made one film together, for which the striking one-sheet is offered here.

• 692 **NO MAN OF HER OWN**, Paramount, 1932, one-sheet, Cond. A, linen backed
41 x 27 in $8,000-10,000

The United States' posters for **Wuthering Heights** are very disappointing. Almost any collector would prefer to have the original Belgian poster offered here. Greta Garbo was the only major female star who easily made the transition from silent films to sound films, achieving equal stardom in both.

• 693 **LOVE BEFORE BREAKFAST**, Universal, 1936, one-sheet, Cond. A, paper backed
41 x 27 in $1,000-1,500

• 694 **WUTHERING HEIGHTS**, Goldwyn, 1939, Belgian poster, Cond. A
33 x 24 in $700-900

• 695 **THE SINGLE STANDARD**, MGM, 1929, one-sheet, Cond. A, linen backed
41 x 27 in $3,000-4,000

• 696 **CAMILLE**, MGM, 1936, jumbo window card, Cond. A
28 x 22 in $2,000-3,000

Born to be Kissed was the original title to **The Girl from Missouri**, and a few window cards with the earlier title were produced.

• 697 **CLEOPATRA**, Paramount, 1934, jumbo window card, Cond. B, paper backed
28 x 22 in $2,000-3,000

• 698 **BORN TO BE KISSED**, MGM, 1934, window card, Cond. A, top trimmed
18 x 14 in $1,000-1,500

• 699 **SHANGHAI EXPRESS**, Paramount, 1932, half-sheet, Cond. B, paper backed
22 x 28 in $2,500-3,500

Marlene Dietrich achieved stardom in a series of films with Josef von Sternberg, including **Shanghai Express**. Later, she worked for another great European director, Ernst Lubitsch, in **Angel**.

ADOLPH ZUKOR presents
MARLENE
DIETRICH
in "ANGEL"
with
HERBERT MARSHALL
MELVYN DOUGLAS
EDWARD EVERETT HORTON · ERNEST COSSART
LAURA HOPE CREWS · HERBERT MUNDIN
Produced and Directed by
ERNST LUBITSCH
Screen Play by SAMSON RAPHAELSON · From the Play by Melchior Lengyel · English play adaptation by Guy Bolton and Russell Medcraft
A PARAMOUNT PICTURE

• 700 **ANGEL**, Paramount, 1937, three-sheet, Cond. B, linen backed
81 x 41 in $6,000-8,000

• 701 **PRIVATE NUMBER**, 20th Century Fox, 1936, three-sheet, Cond. A, linen backed
81 x 41 in $900-1,200

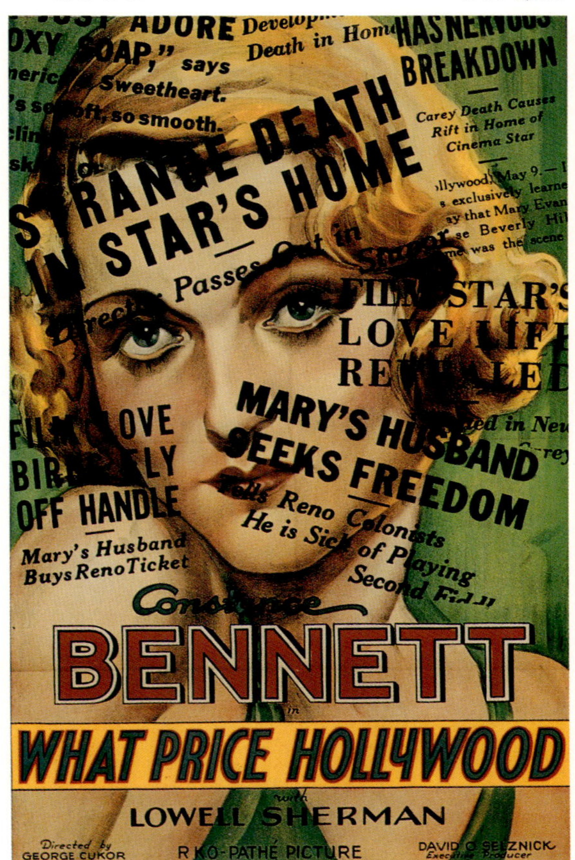

• 702 **WHAT PRICE HOLLYWOOD**, RKO, 1932, one-sheet, Cond. A
41 x 27 in $900-1,200

Although the major studios made forty by sixty silkscreen posters on every film in the 1930s, virtually none are known to have survived. The forty by sixty from **Special Agent** offered here has an striking image of Bette Davis, and is in excellent condition.

• 703 **SPECIAL AGENT**, Warner Brothers, 1935, forty by sixty, Cond. A, unfolded
60 x 40 in $2,000-3,000

Jezebel is the rare case of a great motion picture having an equally great poster image. Most would agree that it is the finest single movie poster image of Bette Davis.

• 704 **JEZEBEL**, Warner Brothers, 1938,
one-sheet, Cond. A, linen backed
41 x 27 in $8,000-10,000

The striking **The Petrified Forest** poster offered here was made by a company in the midwest that in 1935 and 1936 produced its own posters for Hollywood films.

• 705 **JEZEBEL**, Warner Brothers, 1938, window card, Cond. B, paper backed
22 x 14 in $1,500-2,000

• 706 **THE PETRIFIED FOREST**, Warner Brothers, 1936, special poster, Cond. B
60 x 40 in $4,000-6,000

• 707 **THE PRIVATE LIVES OF ELIZABETH AND ESSEX**, Warner Brothers, 1939, Belgian poster, Cond. A, top trimmed
30 x 24 in $700-900

• 708 **STRANGE CARGO**, MGM, 1940, one-sheet, Cond. A
41 x 27 in $400-600

• 709 **GOIN' TO TOWN**, Paramount, 1935, six-sheet, Cond. A (has censor stamps), linen backed
81 x 81 in $5,000-7,000

Mae West was already a legend when she made **Goin' to Town** in 1935. The unknown poster artist who rendered the six-sheet offered here not only captured her likeness exactly, but also created a striking image that embodies West's come-hither sex appeal.

The Bicycle Thief won numerous awards, and posters were immediately issued showing the awards it had won. Consequently, the pre-awards posters, such as the one offered here, are extremely difficult to obtain.

• 710 **THE BICYCLE THIEF,** PDS-ENIC, 1948,
Italian two panel, Cond. A, linen backed
78 x 55 in $8,000-10,000

Federico Fellini made many great films, but his two masterpieces were **La Dolce Vita** and **8 1/2**. Remarkably, an original billboard poster from **La Dolce Vita** has survived, and is offered here.

• 711 **THE MIRACLE IN MILAN**, PDS-ENIC, 1951,
Italian poster, Cond. A, linen backed
55 x 39 in $6,000-8,000

• 712 **8 1/2**, Cineriz, 1963,
Italian poster, Cond. A, linen backed
55 x 39 in $1,000-1,500

• 713 **LA DOLCE VITA**, Riama/Pathe, 1960,
Italian billboard poster, Cond. A
117 x 220 in $8,000-10,000

Los Olvidados is considered to be Luis Bunuel's greatest film, and the rare original Mexican poster for the film is offered here.

• 714 **LA BELLE ET LA BETE**, Paulve, 1946, French two panel, Cond. A, linen backed 63 x 94 in $8,000-10,000

• 715 **THE DISCREET CHARM OF THE BOURGEOISIE**, Silberman, 1972, French poster, Cond. A
32 x 23 in $600-800

• 716 **LOS OLVIDADOS**, Ultramar, 1951, Mexican poster, Cond. A, linen backed
37 x 27 in $1,000-1,500

Great Britain has always had a thriving film industry, led by such great directors as Alexander Korda, David Lean, and Carol Reed. Original English posters from their films are extremely rare.

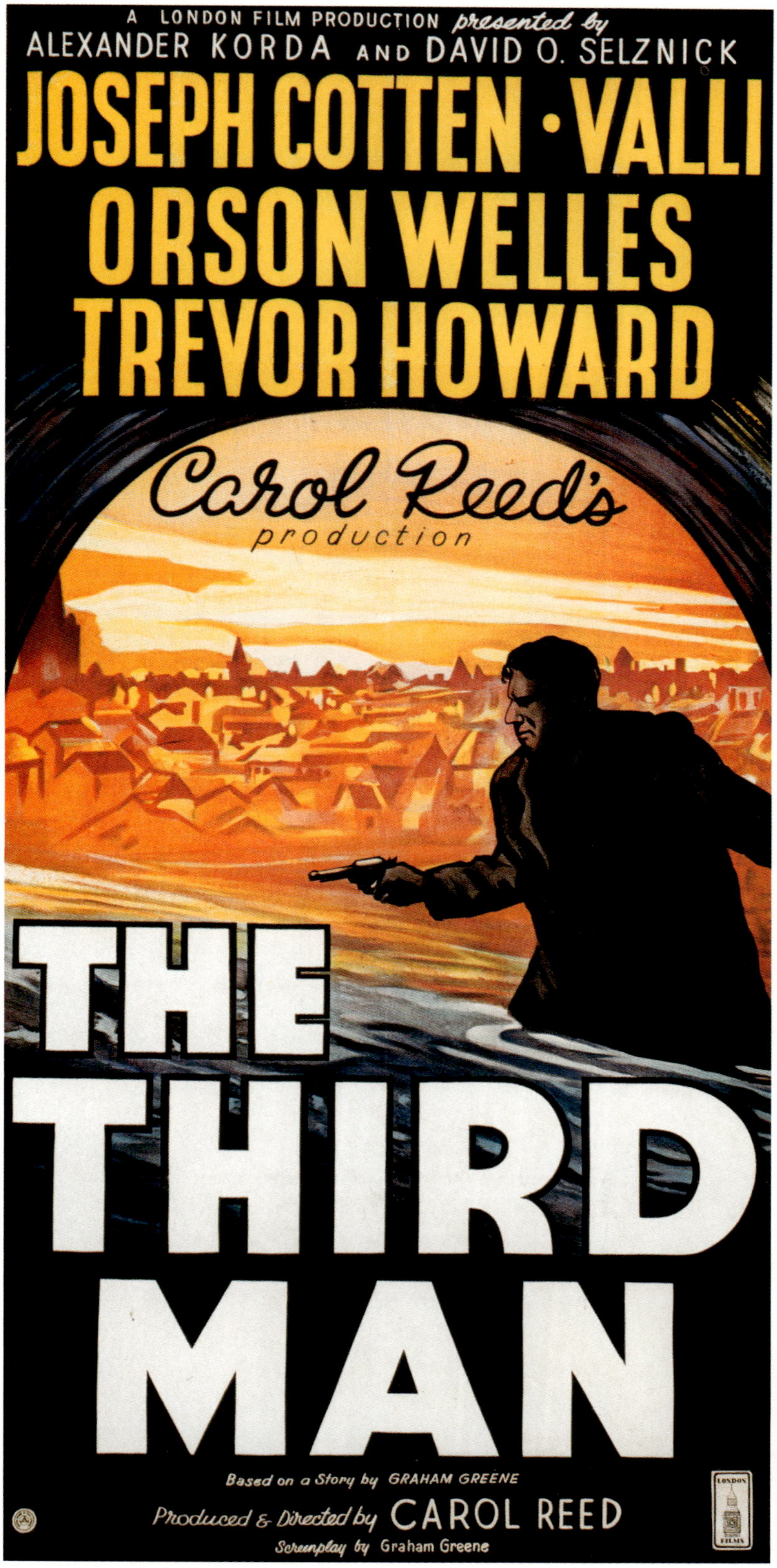

• 717 **THE THIRD MAN**, London Films, 1949, British three-sheet, Cond. B, linen backed
76 x 39 in $1,500-2,000

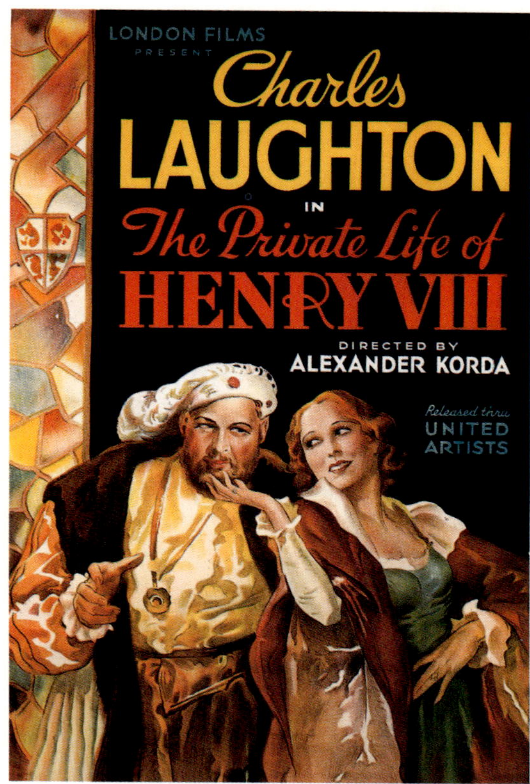

• 718 **THE PRIVATE LIFE OF HENRY VIII**, United Artists, 1933, one-sheet, Cond. A, paper backed
41 x 27 in $4,000-6,000

• 719 **NICHOLAS NICKLEBY**, General film, 1947, British half-sheet, Cond. A
22 x 28 in $500-700

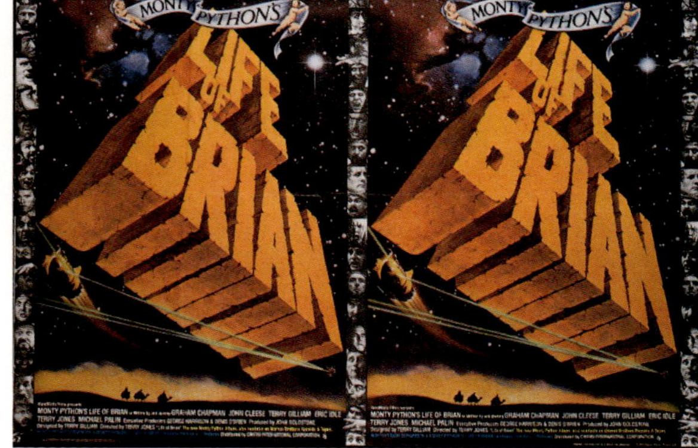

• 720 **LIFE OF BRIAN**, Orion, 1979, British quad, Cond. A
30 x 40 in $200-400

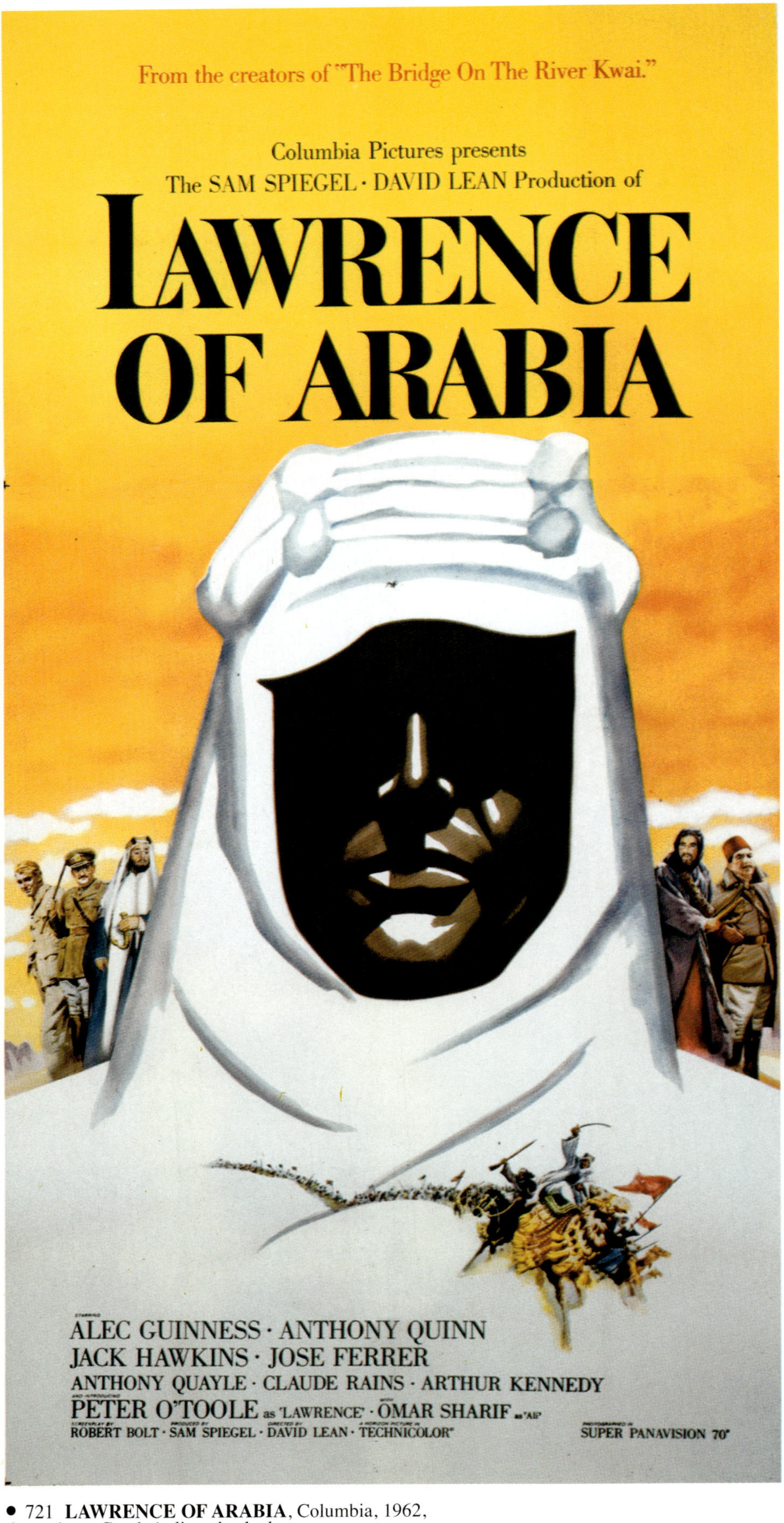
From the creators of "The Bridge On The River Kwai."
Columbia Pictures presents
The SAM SPIEGEL · DAVID LEAN Production of
LAWRENCE OF ARABIA
ALEC GUINNESS · ANTHONY QUINN
JACK HAWKINS · JOSE FERRER
ANTHONY QUAYLE · CLAUDE RAINS · ARTHUR KENNEDY
PETER O'TOOLE as 'LAWRENCE' · OMAR SHARIF as 'ALI'
ROBERT BOLT · SAM SPIEGEL · DAVID LEAN · TECHNICOLOR®
SUPER PANAVISION 70®

• 721 **LAWRENCE OF ARABIA**, Columbia, 1962, three-sheet, Cond. A, linen backed
81 x 41 in $2,000-3,000

BARDOT
HOSSEIN
VADIM
le Repos du Guerrier
FRANSCOPE COULEURS
FRANCIS COSNE
COCINOR
INTERDIT AUX MOINS DE 18 ANS

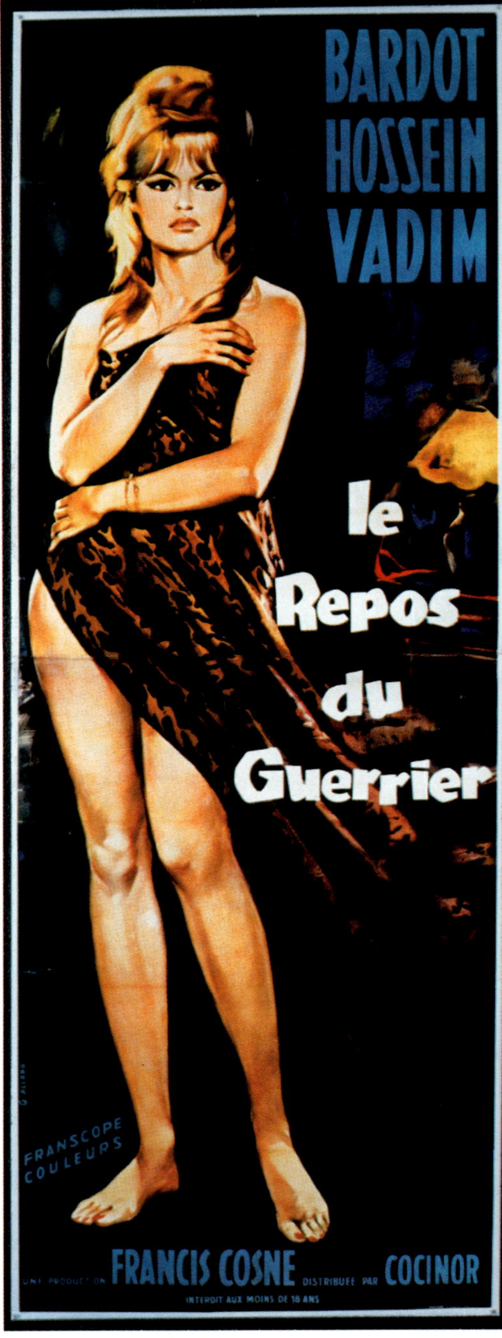

• 722 **LOVE ON A PILLOW**, Concinur, 1962, French door panel, Cond. A, linen backed
123 x 44 in $600-800

Long a director of "little" films, David Lean turned to making "epics". Many consider **Lawrence of Arabia** to be his greatest film..

Marihuana was a low budget film of 1936 that has been reissued periodically over the years. In recent years, it is more viewed as a camp classic.

• 723 **THE THRILL HUNTER**, Columbia, 1933, one-sheet, Cond. A, linen backed
41 x 27 in $700-900

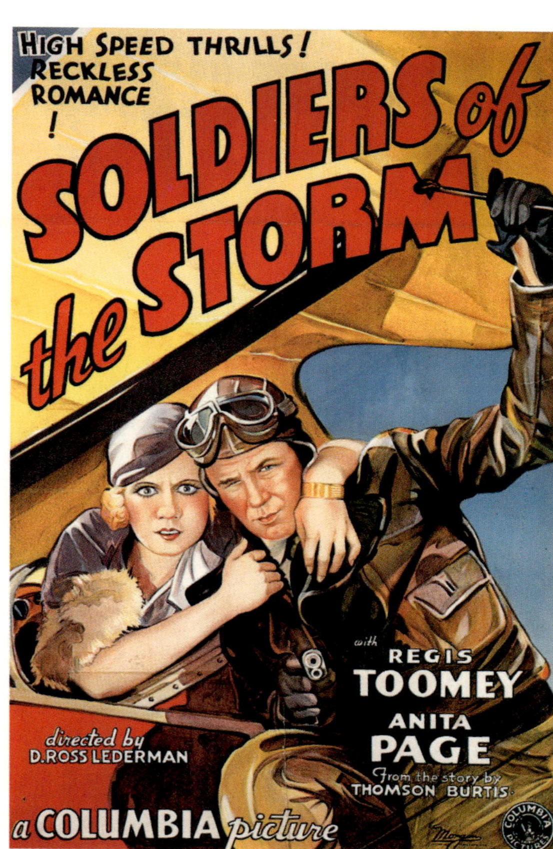

• 724 **SOLDIERS OF THE STORM**, Columbia, 1933, one-sheet, Cond. B
41 x 27 in $700-900

• 725 **MARIHUANA**, Road Show Attractions, 1936, silk banner, Cond. A
60 x 40 in $800-1,000

• 726 **MARIHUANA**, Road Show Attractions, 1936, window card, Cond. A
22 x 14 in $600-800

• 727 **DILLINGER PUBLIC ENEMY NO. 1**, Midland Film, 1934, one-sheet, Cond. A, linen backed
41 x 27 in $1,800-2,400

• 728 **GOING ON TWO**, RKO, 1934, one-sheet, Cond. A, linen backed
41 x 27 in $400-600

• 729 **CHECK AND DOUBLE CHECK**, RKO, 1930, window card, Cond. B
22 x 14 in $1,500-2,000

• 730 **PARAMOUNT ON PARADE**, Paramount, 1930, insert, Cond. B, linen backed
36 x 14 in $500-700

In the days before television, real life events often resulted in documentaries, such as the ones about Dillinger and the Dionne quintuplets offered here. **Check and Double Check** was the only film based on the popular radio show, Amos 'n' Andy.

Clint Eastwood has had two successful film series, one as "The Man With No Name" in the "spaghetti" westerns, and the other as "Dirty Harry" in the series beginning with the film of the same name.

731 **FOR A FEW DOLLARS MORE**, PEA, 1965, forty by sixty, Cond. A, unfolded
60 x 40 in $600-800

732 **THE OUTLAW JOSEY WALES**, Warner Brothers, 1976, forty by sixty, Cond. B, paper backed
60 x 40 in $400-600

733 **THE ENFORCER**, Warner Brothers, 1976, subway poster, Cond. A, linen backed
45 x 60 in $400-600

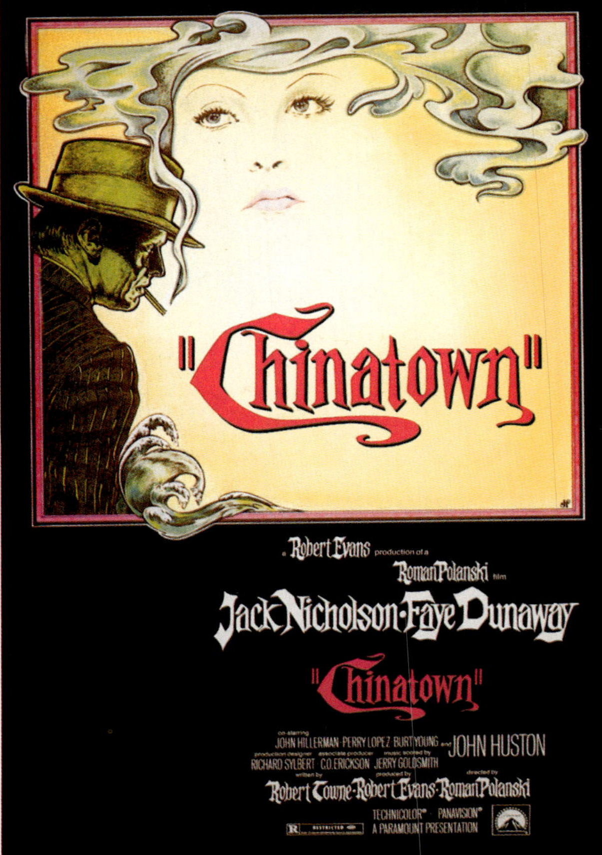

734 **CHINATOWN**, Paramount, 1974,
forty by sixty, Cond. A, unfolded
60 x 40 in $300-500

735 **PULP FICTION**, Miramax, 1994,
advance one-sheet, Cond. A, unfolded
41 x 27 in $100-200

736 **GOLDFINGER**, United Artists, 1964,
two door panels, Cond. A, unfolded
each 60 x 20 in $1,500-2,000

The **Chinatown** movie poster is one of the most popular and sought after images of the 1970s. **Pulp Fiction** seems to be that rare film that has been hailed as an instant classic.

The James Bond films are probably the most enduring and successful film series of recent years, and some of the best and most difficult to obtain Bond posters are offered here.

737 **GOLDFINGER**, United Artists, 1964,
three-sheet, Cond. A, linen backed
81 x 41 in $1,000-1,500

738 **FROM RUSSIA WITH LOVE**, United Artists, 1963,
British quad, Cond A, linen backed
30 x 40 in $1,000-1,500

739 **YOU ONLY LIVE TWICE**, United Artists, 1967,
subway poster, Cond. A
45 x 60 in $600-800

740 **PSYCHO**, Universal, 1960,
lobby card, Cond. A
11 x 14 in $200-400

Perhaps the single most desirable item from **Psycho** is not one of the posters, but the single lobby card that shows the infamous house where "Mother" lived.

The late 1970s and early 1980s gave the world the films of George Lucas and Steven Spielberg, which are among the most entertaining and most profitable films of all time.

741 **THE EMPIRE STRIKES BACK**, 20th Century Fox, 1980, six-sheet, Cond. A, linen backed
81 x 81 in $500-700

742 **JAWS**, Universal, 1975, one-sheet, Cond. A, linen backed
41 x 27 in $300-500

743 **STAR WARS**, 20th Century Fox, 1977, forty by sixty, Cond. A, unfolded
60 x 40 in $300-500

744 **RAIDERS OF THE LOST ARK**, Paramount, 1981, forty by sixty, Cond. A, unfolded, 60 x 40 in $300-500

While **Clockwork Orange** was a masterful, yet deeply disturbing film, many filmmakers imitated only the excessive violence, and the modern horror film was born, with such films as **Halloween**, **Friday the 13th**, and **A Nightmare on Elm Street**.

745 **HALLOWEEN**, Falcon, 1978, one-sheet, Cond. A, unfolded
41 x 27 in $200-400

746 **FRIDAY THE 13TH,** Paramount, 1980, one-sheet, Cond. A, unfolded
41 x 27 in $100-200

747 **A NIGHTMARE ON ELM STREET,** New Line, 1984, one-sheet, Cond. B, linen backed 41 x 27 in $200-400

748 **CLOCKWORK ORANGE**, Warner Brothers, 1971, six-sheet, Cond. A, linen backed
81 x 81 in $800-1,200

The 1970s included many of the films of Woody Allen, culminating in one of his best and most personal films, **Manhattan**. 1975 brought **One Flew Over the Cuckoo's Nest**, from which a rare pre-Academy Award one-sheet is offered here.

749 **THE BLUES BROTHERS**, Universal, 1980, Australian one-sheet, Cond. A
41 x 27 in $400-600

750 **SUPERSTAR**, Marilyn Lewis, 1991, one-sheet, Cond. A, unfolded
41 x 27 in $100-200

751 **ONE FLEW OVER THE CUCKOO'S NEST**, United Artists, 1975, one-sheet, Cond. A, linen backed
41 x 27 in $400-600

752 **MANHATTAN**, United Artists, 1979, one-sheet, Cond. A
41 x 27 in $200-400

The 1980s brought such varying comedic films as **Airplane**, with zany Mad Magazine humor, **The Blues Brothers** with broad slapstick, and **Diner**, a nostalgic look back at how we acted in simpler times.

753 **IT'S A MAD, MAD, MAD, MAD WORLD**, United Artists, 1963, thirty by forty, Cond. A, unfolded
40 x 30 in $200-400

754 **AIRPLANE**, Paramount, 1980, one-sheet, Cond. A
41 x 27 in $100-200

755 **PINK FLAMINGOS**, Saliva Films, 1972, special poster, Cond. A, unfolded
17 x 12 in $200-400

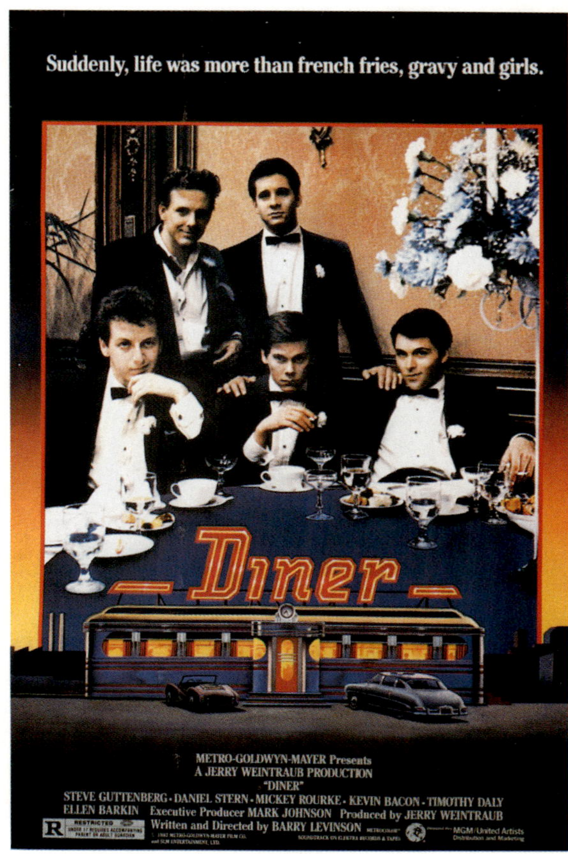

756 **DINER**, MGM/United Artists, 1982, forty by sixty, Cond. A, unfolded
60 x 40 in $200-400

Steven Spielberg struck out with **1941**, a broad comedy, but rebounded with his greatest success in **E.T. The Extra Terrestrial**. **Raging Bull** was chosen as the best film of the 1980s by Premiere Magazine.

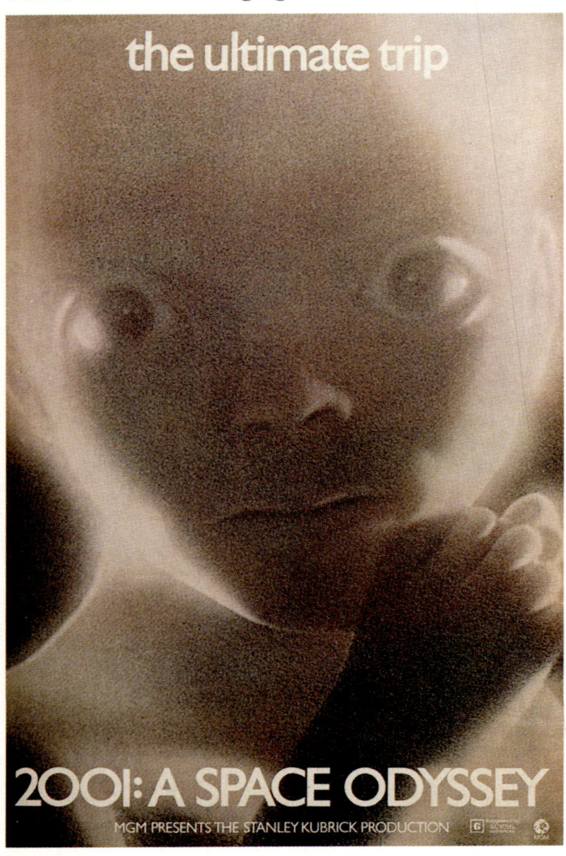

757 **2001: A SPACE ODYSSEY**, MGM, 1971 reissue, forty by sixty, Cond. A, unfolded
60 x 40 in $400-600

758 **E.T. THE EXTRA TERRESTRIAL**, Universal, 1982, advance one-sheet, Cond. A, unfolded
41 x 27 in $300-500

759 **RAGING BULL**, United Artists, 1980, advance one-sheet, Cond. A, unfolded
41 x 27 in $200-300

760 **1941**, Columbia/Universal, 1979, advance one-sheet, Cond. A, unfolded
41 x 27 in $200-300

761 **BATMAN**, 20th Century Fox, 1966,
forty by sixty, Cond. B, unfolded
60 x 40 in $500-700

762 **THE MAN CALLED FLINTSTONE**, Columbia, 1966,
set of eight lobby cards (one pictured), Cond. A
each 11 x 14 in $200-400

763 **BATMAN RETURNS,** Warner Brothers, 1992,
set of three subway posters, Cond. A, unfolded
each 45 x 60 in $300-500

The Batman TV show spawned a feature film version in 1966. In the 1990s, there is a new Batman craze, including the 1992 film, **Batman Returns.**

The 1970s saw many dark films which turned into huge successes. The one-sheet for **The French Connection** offered here is the "B-style", which is extremely rare.

764 **THE GODFATHER, PART II**, Paramount, 1974, advance one-sheet, Cond. A, linen backed
41 x 27 in $300-500

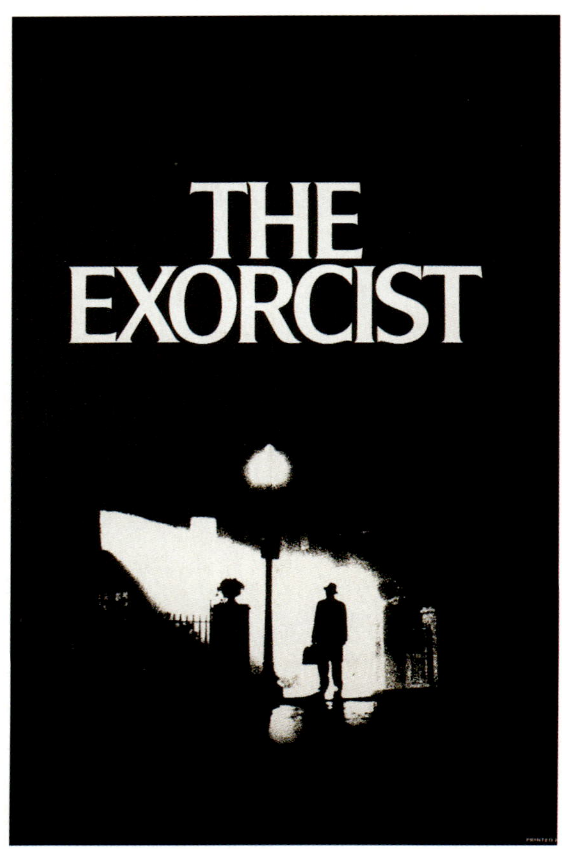

765 **THE EXORCIST**, Warner Brothers, 1973, special poster, Cond. A, paper backed
25 x 19 in $200-400

766 **THE FRENCH CONNECTION**, 20th Century Fox, 1971, one-sheet, Cond. A, linen backed
41 x 27 in $500-700

767 **TAXI DRIVER**, Columbia, 1976, forty by sixty, Cond. A, unfolded
60 x 40 in $300-500

The 1960s was a decade in which the studio system and the way they made films was brought down, largely by the success of independent filmmakers such as Russ Meyer and Peter Fonda.

768 **LOLITA**, MGM, 1962,
British quad, Cond. A, linen backed
30 x 40 in $500-700

769 **MOTORPSYCHO!**, Eve Production, 1965,
one-sheet, Cond. A
41 x 27 in $200-400

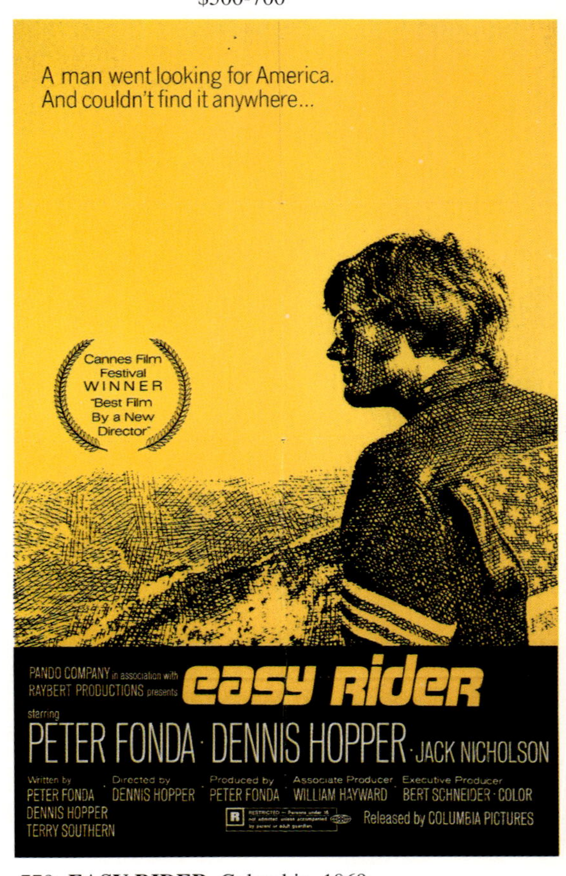

770 **EASY RIDER**, Columbia, 1969,
one-sheet, Cond. A
41 x 27 in $200-400

The early 1980s saw a continuation of the trend which had begun in the 1970s, where dark and disturbing films could achieve great success, if they were made by the best filmmakers.

771 **APOCALYPSE NOW**, United Artists, 1979, one-sheet, Cond. A, unfolded
41 x 27 in $200-400

772 **BLADE RUNNER**, Warner Brothers, 1982, forty by sixty, Cond. A, unfolded
60 x 40 in $200-400

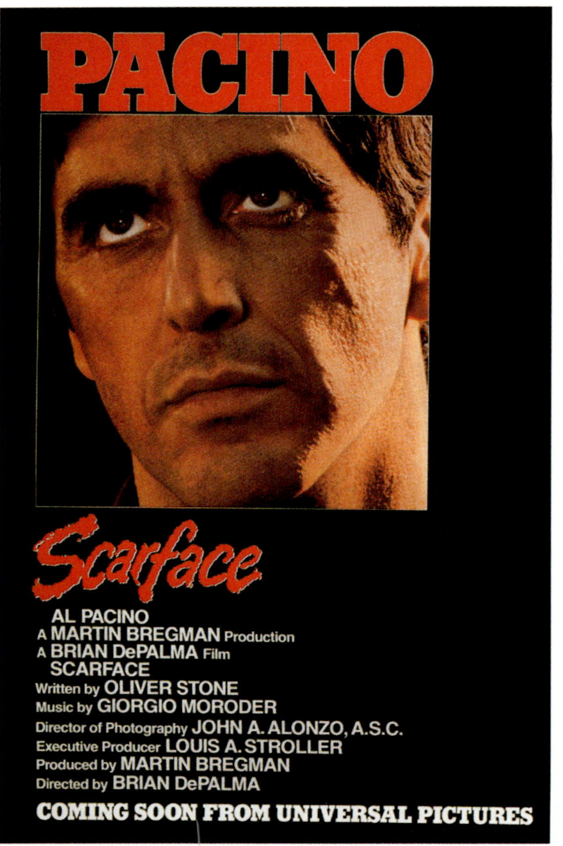

773 **SCARFACE**, Universal, 1983, advance one-sheet, Cond. A, unfolded
41 x 27 in $300-500

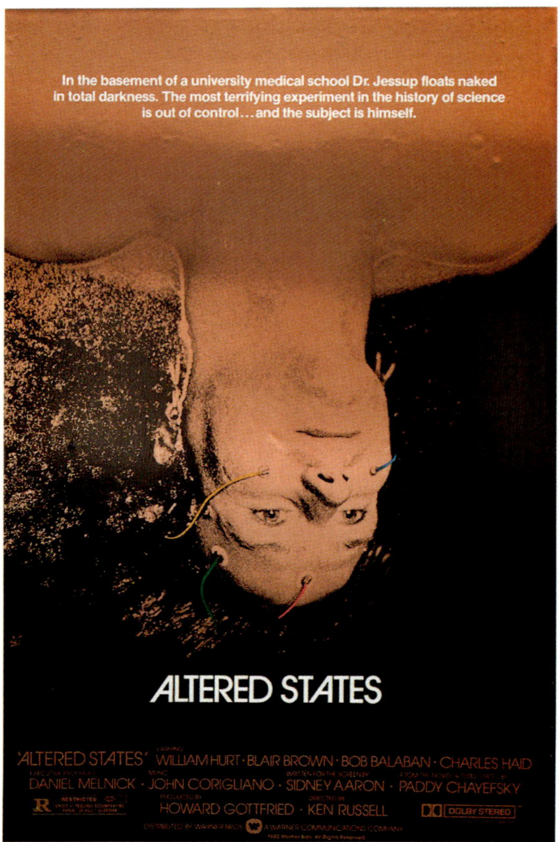

774 **ALTERED STATES**, Warner Brothers, 1980, copper foil poster, Cond. A, unfolded
39 x 25 in $100-200 **END OF SALE**

ROCK AND POP CINEMA POSTERS INDEX

CLASSIC CINEMA POSTERS INDEX

CLASSIC CINEMA POSTERS INDEX (Continued)

ABSENTEE BIDS FORM

To allow time for processing, absentee bids should be received at least 24 hours before the sale begins. Christie's will confirm all bids received by fax by return fax. If you have not received our confirmation within one business day, please resubmit your bid(s) or contact:
Bid Department. Tel: (310) 275 5534 Fax (310) 275 9748.
During exhibition and sale you may also call or fax:
Tel: (310) 657 1003 Fax (310) 657 1881

Billing Name (please print):..

Address:..

....

City:..ZIP code:..........................

State:.. Fax:..................................

Tel. (Daytime):..

(Evening):..

Signature: ....

Client Number (if applicable): ....

SALE TITLE **Rock, Pop, and Classic Cinema Posters**

DATE **Sunday, 15 December 1996**
at 4.00p.m. & 6.00p.m.

SALE NO. **7943**

SALE **Murray Feldman Gallery**
Pacific Design Center

ADDRESS **8687 Melrose Avenue**
Los Angeles, CA 90069

[Dealers: Billing name and address should agree with your state or local sales tax exemption certificate. Invoices cannot be changed after they have been printed.]

I request that Christie's enters bids on the following lots up to the maximum price I have indicated for each lot. I understand that if my bid is successful, the purchase price will be the sum of my final bid plus a premium of 15% of the final bid price up to and including $50,000 and 10% of the amount above $50,000 ("buyer's premium") and any applicable state or local sales or use tax.

I understand that Christie's executes absentee bids as a convenience for clients and is not responsible for inadvertently failing to execute bids or for errors relating to execution of bids. On my behalf, Christie's will try to purchase these lots for the lowest possible price, taking into account the reserve and other bids.

If identical absentee bids are left, Christie's will give precedence to the first one received. All successful bids are subject to the terms of the Conditions of Sale and Limited Warranty printed in the front of each Christie's catalogue.

PLEASE PRINT CLEARLY IN BLOCK LETTERS

Lot no (in numerical order)	Price bid $ (excluding buyer's premium)

Lot no (in numerical order)	Price bid $ (excluding buyer's premium)

To be sure that bids will be accepted and delivery of lots not delayed, bidders not yet known to Christie's should supply a bank reference.

Name of Bank(s):...

Address of Bank(s):...

....

....

Account Number(s): ....

Name of Account Officer(s):...

Bank Telephone Number:...